T0165210

# The French Stethoscope

*How a French Doctor turned life challenges into opportunities and deep appreciation*

By

## Chris Elisabeth Gilbert, M.D, Ph.D.

iUniverse, Inc.
New York   Bloomington

The French Stethoscope
How a French Doctor turned life challenges into opportunities and
deep appreciation

*Copyright © 2010 by* Chris Elisabeth Gilbert, M.D, Ph.D.

*All rights reserved. No part of this book may be used or reproduced by any means,
graphic, electronic, or mechanical, including photocopying, recording, taping or by
any information storage retrieval system without the written permission of the publisher
except in the case of brief quotations embodied in critical articles and reviews.*

*iUniverse books may be ordered through booksellers or by contacting:*

*iUniverse
1663 Liberty Drive
Bloomington, IN 47403
www.iuniverse.com
1-800-Authors (1-800-288-4677)*

*Because of the dynamic nature of the Internet, any Web addresses or links contained in this
book may have changed since publication and may no longer be valid. The views expressed
in this work are solely those of the author and do not necessarily reflect the views of the
publisher, and the publisher hereby disclaims any responsibility for them.*

*ISBN: 978-1-4502-4814-3 (sc)*
*ISBN: 978-1-4502-4815-0 (ebook)*

*Printed in the United States of America*

*iUniverse rev. date: 9/9/2010*

In medicine there is no guarantee. The information provided in this book is offered for educational purposes only.

The information in this book does not create a physician-patient relationship between you and Dr. Gilbert.

Dr. Gilbert does not guarantee the accuracy or completeness of any information available in this book.

You must check with your personal physician to assess whether suggestions herein are appropriate for you since results will vary among individuals and there could be substantial risks involved.

# Acknowlegments

In memory of my wonderful husband, Steve, my best friend, my Prince Charming, the Love of my Life. Steve, your intelligence, strength and sense of humor brightened each of my days during 12 awesome years of marriage.

In memory of my perfect father, Jacques. Dad, your wisdom and sense of humor brightened my entire childhood. Thank you for teaching me how to be a great physician and a good human being.

To my amazing mother, Jacqueline. Your inner and outer beauty shine in my heart everyday. Thank you for teaching me how to listen to people and to respect everybody regardless. Thank you for your Unconditional Love which gave me the strength to be who I am.

To all my friends and family members whose support has been strong throughout the years.

To Doctors Without Borders which allowed me to donate my time, knowledge and love to so many refugees all over the world.

To Club Med which allowed me to express my two true passions: medicine and acting.

To all my patients: this memoir is what I would like to share with each of you. This is the story of my life to date and what I learned from it.

I hope that you will find information, inspiration and insight that will influence your own outlook on life.

Many thanks to all the people who participated in the editing and photography for this book: Above all, my husband Steve Chmura, my father Jacques Gilbert and my mother Jacqueline Gilbert. Also Kim Chmura, Barbara Cole, Richard and Christine Forest, Evelyn Goodwin and Pierre Colin.

Note: In this memoir, some names were changed to respect people's privacy

In loving memory of

my father Jacques

and my husband Steve

# Contents

# List of Illustrations

# Introduction

In my busy private medical practice, I always tell my patients to live their lives to their fullest. Life is too short and too precious to spend it complaining about the place you live or the mate you are married to. Life is an amazing gift that should be appreciated to its fullest.

How do you do that?

Well, here is my own story.

In this memoir you will know how I did it. How I dealt with my own illnesses (scoliosis and lymphocytic colitis) and surgeries, how I worked in refugee camps in Asia and Africa in sometimes very hard conditions and still appreciated life to its fullest.

I explain my fight against my father's colon cancer then metastatic colon cancer to his liver and brain.

I also explain my fight against my husband's deadly brain cancer also called glioblastoma multiforme.

Above all, this book is a celebration of Life and the pursuit of Happiness. It will relate how I decided to move to my dream country and settled in my dream town, how I pursued my dream work and how I searched for and found my soul mate.

Yes, life is made of a series of ups and downs for everybody. The key is always to look at the positive side of things, always search deep inside for what your dreams and aspirations are and go for them.

Here are the first 50 years of my life. I hope this memoir will give you inspiration, will and strength to celebrate your own Life and the pursuit of your own Happiness.

# Chapter 1
# Starting with pain

## *March 1968*

"Ouch!!! Ouch!!! Stop!!! Please stop!!! It hurts!!! Ouch!!! Ouch!!!"

I screamed forever. I thought I was going to die. I thought my head was going to break loose from my body. I tried to resist but I couldn't, they were too strong. I promised myself that if I was ever going to survive, I … forget it, I couldn't even think. I was in too much pain.

Then finally, they stopped pulling and I started looking around: one huge man who was at least 6'3" and 300 lbs was pulling my hips and feet one direction while another man equally huge was pulling my head in the other direction.

It was the latest approved treatment for scoliosis…. I was 11 years old and was starting my growth spur, heading towards puberty. It was the only way doctors knew at that time to prevent my scoliosis to get worse. After pulling on my head and feet in opposite directions, I felt some warm thick sticky material being wrapped around my body. The men had proceeded to make a body cast from my neck to my hips. As they were finishing the cast, they pulled out a piece of gauze that was attached to my back and in doing so, they tore my skin open underneath the cast. It hurt so much that I screamed and screamed but nobody listened to my complaint. I was only a kid. I was going to stay in this cast for 6 months! Yes, the same damn cast for 6 months! With an open wound underneath the cast! My God was this uncomfortable! My God was the open wound painful, especially when it later got infected! Of course nobody would listen to me when I was saying that something was hurting underneath my body cast. Only when the wound started to be so infected that it would smell so bad that eventually my doctor decided to cut a window in the cast to see what was underneath. He was horrified to discover a very deep wound that was so deeply infected that you could smell it at 100 feet. It was a relief to finally get it treated. This is when I started to realize that life is priceless and this is when I promised myself that when I would get out of this cast, I would enjoy every single minute of my life. I would go to medical school to become a physician like my Dad. This way, nobody could harm me any more. I would have total control.

Because I had suffered so much, my parents got me a dog, a little black poodle that we named Skiwi. Skiwi was so adorable, always in a good mood, always ready to play and cuddle. He was the perfect dog for me.

My Dad made jokes all the time. He was such a pleasure to be with. When we were at the kitchen table, eating dinner, he would peel an orange during the time my mother was preparing the next dish, and then he would reconstitute it as if it were intact (in reality, it was an empty orange peel) and would put it on Mom's plate. We would look at each other with kinky smiles, anticipating the delightful reaction of Mom. Five minutes later, when she would come back to the table, she would notice the orange and grab it to put it back in the refrigerator. She would jump and scream with surprise, when her finger would go right through the empty peel. Dad and I would laugh endlessly at her reaction. This would work each time.

We would go out to eat about once a month and Dad's favorite joke was to imitate the meow of a cat, first very softly, then louder and without moving either his lips or his face. Then, he would look around and say: "I hear a cat, does anybody have a cat?" All the other tables would look around too but nobody would find any cat. Then 10 minutes later, he would start again. It was so hilarious!!! Mom and I were laughing so much! Then, he would start telling all kinds of jokes. That's why his patients loved him so much. First, he was an excellent physician, then he had a great sense of humor and he genuinely cared for each of his patients. He would bring home wild turkeys (offered to him by one of his patients who was a hunter), raspberries (another one was growing them in her garden) and many more goodies.

After being in private practice and on call every night for 10 years, he started getting tired of prescribing medications with a lot of side effects and became interested in homeopathy and acupuncture. He started studying again, took the homeopathy and acupuncture exams, then shifted his practice from general medicine to mostly homeopathy and acupuncture. I was 13 years old at that time.

I loved watching American movies and I fell in love with Los Angeles and Hollywood. My dream was to become an actress and live in LA. I loved being on stage. Unfortunately, when I told this to my parents, the answer I received was: "Acting is not a real job and signing you up for acting classes is not an option at this time. You need to choose a real career first and then, once you have a real career, you can study acting". I was a good daughter - I didn't insist.

I started being curious about medicine and asking Dad a lot of questions - about how the body was functioning. At the beginning, he answered my questions but as they were becoming more and more numerous, he told me that I was too young to understand. I reacted right away saying that if this was so, I would go to medical school. He then proceeded to tell me that being a physician was not a profession for women. It was much too tiring and I would have to work way too many hours to be compatible with a family life. He said: "You should be a teacher like your Mom!!!" That's when I made up my mind to go to Medical School.

My mother was definitely a teacher. She was the most beautiful woman I had ever seen, blond with a perfect trendy hairstyle, strikingly beautiful green-blue-grey eyes, gorgeous smile, slim and always impeccably and femininely dressed. She was the kind of woman people would turn around to look at. She loved teaching. Since I was an only child, all her efforts were unfortunately concentrated on me which I resented a lot at the time. Now, I am thankful for this because without her, I would never have made it through medical school. But at the time, it would annoy me to no end! "Chris, did you do your homework?" No, Mom, I want to play first" Oh, no, no, no, let's look at your homework"…this was the same thing everyday. I got used to it.

My parents genuinely loved each other. They were always holding hands and telling each other how much they loved each other. I don't think I ever heard them argue. They had a very traditional marriage with my Dad bringing money home and my Mom doing the grocery shopping, cooking, washing clothes and ironing. They were very happy and showed me how happy a marriage could be. It was a great example. It made me want to marry some time and have the same kind of marriage,…except for the ironing part which I hated – more on that later.

I was an A-student in high school and as I had promised myself, I applied to Medical School. To my Dad's surprise, I was accepted at one of the most prestigious Medical Schools of Paris. That is when I proudly bought the stethoscope that was going to accompany me in all my future adventures. At that time, my female hormones started hitting a very high level - all I wanted to do was play and explore being with boys - all my parents were allowing me to do was study and be by myself. I was a good daughter, so I studied and studied and studied. I got excellent grades. The more I was drawn to boys and playing, the more I was studying to keep my mind off those disturbing thoughts. Needless to say I studied extremely hard and all the time. I couldn't wait to finish medical school to be finally able to play.

I was finishing Medical School in Paris when Paul whom I was studying with fell in love with me. Paul was a handsome, tall man with beautiful brown eyes hidden behind trendy glasses. I was attracted to him but I was certainly not ready to marry either him or anybody else at that time. After being tied up so many years at home studying, I wanted to travel - I was thirsty for adventure.

I was ready to explore all the possible countries on earth, all the different civilizations. As a matter of fact, I had just found an ad for a hospital in Martinique in the French Caribbean, looking for medical students willing to stay one year for an internship (6 months in internal medicine and 6 months in Ob-Gyn). Martinique had become a region of France in 1974. Lying in the heart of the Caribbean Archipelago, it was one of the many islands making up the group of the lesser Antilles between Dominica North and Saint Lucia South. It was a very small island, only 50 miles by 22 miles with a tropical climate. I was very tempted.

When Paul proposed to me, I had to say "no". I tried to explain to him that my "no" had nothing to do with him. I was simply not ready to marry anyone. I was just starting my life. My eyes were wide open and I was like a bird coming out of 20 years of living in a cage. I was ready to open my wings, fly away and explore the world. I tried to explain this to him over and over again, but he couldn't understand. The following day, as I was dropping by his house to see how he was doing, I found him unconscious on his bed with empty bottles of medications on his bed stand. I called 911. Ten minutes later, the paramedics were there and we got him transferred to the nearest emergency room. After a gastric lavage, he regained consciousness. After a few days in the hospital, he returned home but refused to talk to me. In fact, he hasn't spoken to me since then. He probably never understood me.

I decided to contact the hospital in Martinique to see if the intern position was still available. It was!!! I immediately sent my application and was accepted shortly afterwards. This was going to be the beginning of one of the most exciting parts of my life - traveling.

Dad and I (4 months old)

Mom and I (5 years old)

My dog Skiwi and I (13 years old)

I was 16 years old

Mom, Dad and I (20 years old)

# Chapter 2
# The beginning of freedom

## *September 1980*

I was so excited! My heavy suitcase was packed with all my medical books and favorite clothes! I was on my way to the airport! In 9 hours, I would land in Martinique were I knew no one and would work in Lamentin Hospital for one year. It was a complete open door to the absolute thrilling and delightful unknown. It was heavenly!!! I had no idea where I would stay although the hospital said that I could use one of their rooms as a bedroom. As we boarded the plane, I found myself sitting near an attractive young man, Eric. We started talking. His parents were the owners of the Culinary Institute of Martinique. We instantly became friends. He was tall, slim, and very mature for his age - 17. He started telling me about all the great things to do on the island. It sounded wonderful. 7 hours later, as we landed in Fort-de-France, my body experienced for the first time the very hot and humid weather I would come to love so much. It was 95 degrees F. ! Such a difference from the cold and windy Parisian weather! I felt immediately at ease. I met Eric's parents who were at the airport to pick him up - delightful people, very open and warm. They offered to drop me off at the hospital. I gladly accepted. As we were driving, it got dark outside. I could see we were arriving in a poor suburb. Then a hospital...dark, dirty,...the person at the gate knew nothing about a room for me. It was Friday night. He said that everyone was gone for the day and that tomorrow, being the week-end, there wouldn't be anyone before Monday to authorize my room at the hospital. "Drop by Monday morning at 8:00 am" he said "Maybe somebody will know about you then". I got scared. It was not the modern hospital I imagined. It was a very old hospital in a poor area of the town of Lamentin.

Seeing how scared I was, Eric's parents offered: "Why don't you stay with us tonight and this week-end? You can relax with us. Eric's sister is not home this week. You can use her bedroom. Then, on Monday, you can come back here". I accepted right away. It was so kind of them to invite me into their home. After all, they had just met me. They took me to their home in Fort-de-France. It was a beautiful modern home with air conditioning. My room was very homey. I had a super week-end. Eric took me everywhere on his moped and we had a super time. Food was unbelievable. Imagine eating at the culinary institute everyday! Wonderful! I was so grateful to them. They had become my new family!

Monday morning arrived all too fast, and it was time for me to pack and return to Lamentin Hospital. I was shedding tears as I said goodbye to my new friends. They offered me to visit again the following week-end. I gladly accepted. Half an hour later, their driver took me to Lamentin. Finally I was seeing everything by daytime. The town of Lamentin was a poor area, definitely poorer that Fort-de-France but it was colorful. There were a lot of shops. When we arrived at the hospital, someone directed me to the office for new interns. There, a lady took me to my patient's room which would be my bedroom for the year and then to the Ob-Gyn department for the beginning of my rotation. There was no air conditioning in the hospital, but this was not uncomfortable for me, as my body really enjoyed tropical heat and humidity. There were tons of huge cockroaches running everywhere on the island, and plenty of mosquitoes as well. My bedroom was small but it had everything I needed. Fortunately, it was in a quiet area of the hospital. It was very scary the first day, then a little less scary the second and by the third day, I was completely comfortable with the place. I knew I could adapt to just about anything. I was young, flexible and open to new experiences. This definitely qualified as a new experience!

This was also the first time I was living without my parents. That alone made it very exciting. I was finally free to play and explore life. There was nobody anymore telling me what to do and what not to do. It was AWESOME!!! I was in heaven.

My academic year was divided into 2 parts. The first 6 months, I was an intern in the Ob-Gyn department. The next 6 months, I was to be an intern in the Internal Medicine department. Two other interns were girls like me, and the rest were VAT which stands for Voluntaire Aide Technique. Those were young French male physicians fulfilling their French military obligation. They were all very handsome men, working as surgeons, pediatricians, obstetricians and internal medicine physicians. It was wonderful to be one of the very few privileged women interns in the hospital. It was also wonderful to be 23 years old and full of energy. The call schedule was very easy - it was possible to sleep sometimes the whole night without being called. The island of Martinique was really beautiful. The vegetation was luxurious. The weather was great, just the way I liked it.

The first night I was on call, the E.R. called me for a 10 year old girl who was having abdominal distension and abdominal cramps. When I arrived at her bedside, I was surprised to find a beautiful native girl from Martinique with a large belly. She said that she started gaining weight about 9 months prior little by little but that "yesterday, the abdominal cramps started". She felt very bloated and the cramps were starting to be unbearable. That's when she decided to come to the hospital. When I put my hands on her belly, I found a large abdomen with a huge uterus. Inside her uterus, something was moving and kicking- she was pregnant!!! I did a vaginal exam which showed me that her cervix was almost completely dilated. She was ready to deliver. I was surprised and by the way, so was she. She was only 10 years old, ready to deliver and still had no idea that she was pregnant! I took her to the delivery room and within the next 5 hours, she delivered a healthy baby boy.

During my 6 months in the Ob-Gyn department, I had several cases like this. Young girls not taking any contraception (at 10 to 13 years old, who would?) would get pregnant by local boys. They would continue living at their mother's house, not saying a word to anyone. They would gain weight little by little over the months, not aware they were pregnant and then would come to the E.R. complaining of stomach cramps after 9 months. It was the shock of their life: coming in the hospital for stomach pain and leaving the hospital with a baby!

In Lamentin, Martinique, a lot of women were having children out of wedlock. The more children they had, the more money they received from the French government. Martinique had a high unemployment rate - a lot of men were not working. The weather was very hot and rum was cheap and readily available. As a matter of fact, a delicious rum was made on the island and it was a ritual to have a "Ti Punch" before dinners.

The town of Lamentin was very small but it did have one long commercial street with plenty of shops. I would walk along the streets almost daily. Women were home taking care of children or working, men were outside watching people walking by. They would whistle at pretty young women who walked by. A lot of them smelled like alcohol. I got used to it. Nothing bad ever happened to me. They would whistle at me and sometimes follow me a few feet but nothing more. I felt safe in Lamentin. Most of my week-ends were spent at the Culinary Institute of Martinique where I was happy to be with my new "family". It was a great break from the hospital.

I loved the weather which was very hot and sunny every day. Then sometimes, out of the blue, some heavy black clouds would come and it would rain heavily for about 15 minutes. Then all the sudden, the rain would stop and the sky would become blue again. It was wonderful. On my days off, I explored the island. I went North through the gorgeous tropical rain forest to the Montagne Pelee, a dormant volcano at 4,586 feet. I walked along the most magestic Salines Beach at the Southern tip of the island, swam in front of the Diamond rock and collected beautiful white sand from Saint-Anne beach.

The first 6 months went by very fast. I learned how to do pelvic ultrasounds and became very good at them. I learned how to deliver babies and became very good at it. We had a special cook for us interns and her food was fabulous. We became friends quickly. She would cook all the island specialties for us. Most of all, her fish "accras" and her blood sausages were delicious. Fish "accras" are deep fried very spicy little balls of fish mixed with a batter. They were so good and I ate so many of them that I gained 8 pounds during the first 6 months. To this day, this is the heaviest I have ever been. My normal weight had always been 108 lbs (I am still 108 pounds to this day). Well I weighed up to 116 pounds which was really heavy for me. Everybody would comment: "Chris, you're gaining weight!" Annoyed, I would answer: "Yes, I am, I am trying to put on as much weight as I can". This wasn't true but I had to make them shut up and that sentence would work. In reality, I was trying to lose weight without success. Those fish "accras" were simply too delicious.

Soon after, it was time to change rotation. My second rotation was in Internal Medicine. It was exciting too - although I didn't care for the attending physician. At the end of the year, I knew I had to write a Ph.D. dissertation and I had to find a subject for it. I went down to the nephrology unit and met the nephrology attending physician who was just charming. He suggested I write my dissertation on "Peritoneal Dialysis in Lamentin Hospital - 5 year summary". I accepted and soon afterwards, I would spend all my free time in the nephrology department studying data and writing my dissertation. This made the rest of the year go even faster. I didn't see time go by. Before I knew it, it was time to fly back to Paris. My year of internship was over. I had to finish my dissertation, submit it to my faculty to obtain at the same time both my M. D. and Ph. D.

My last day, I said goodbye to everybody. I had tears in my eyes. I said goodbye to the wonderful cook and her delicious "accras". I said goodbye to my new family. It was hard to leave a place where I had just spent a year but more adventures were ahead of me. I boarded the plane to return to Paris.

# Chapter 3
# The most painful surgery ever!

Paris, France, December 1981: That day was a big day. I was so excited. I had to present my dissertation in front of all my faculty professors. What if they rejected it? After all I created it in a small hospital overseas, not in a main faculty hospital on the mainland. I had no time to think any more. I had to go. Whatever would happen, would happen.

After one hour of metro ride, I entered a large room where many of my faculty professors were sitting. I sat down facing them and presented my Ph.D. dissertation. They asked a lot of questions on the patients I saw and on my life in Martinique. To my relief, after one hour, they congratulated me for they were awarding me a Ph.D. I was really happy, thanked them, shook their hands and left. Outside the door my parents were waiting for me. I had a big smile on my face. We went to a nice restaurant to celebrate.

Soon after, I received my official Ph.D. certificate and official M.D. certificate. This was a huge achievement. The question was: what was I going to do next?

At that time, Dad was seeing patients only 3 days a week and was completely booked well in advance. He had switched his general medicine practice to a mostly Homeopathy and Acupuncture practice. After working 10 years as a general practitioner, he had become interested in alternative medicine and had resumed his medical studies. When I was in medical school, he was also studying and preparing for his

Homeopathy and Acupuncture exams. Dad was incredibly smart and a very good man. All his patients loved him. He was concerned about the side effects of conventional medications. Most of his patients didn't need them. As he started prescribing homeopathic medicines and using acupuncture, most of his patients suddenly got better. They had no more side effects from the "meds". Everybody was happy. Dad started to have more and more patients and pretty soon, he was booked solid one month in advance.

He treated Mom and me with Homeopathy too - I loved it. As soon as I had the first symptom of anything, he would come to me with the appropriate homeopathic medicine. A few hours later, I was usually cured. His biggest success with me was with my hay fever. We had tried traditional medicine with allergy shots which were painful and did not work. I hated shots! Dad decided to stop the shots and started me on a 100 % homeopathic treatment with Histaminum 30C. A few months later, my hay fever was under control. I was thrilled and very thankful. Although I had never really studied Homeopathy, I was completely in favor of it.

Well, remember Dad was working only 3 days a week. He was looking for another physician to work the other 3 days of the week, using the same office. He offered me the position. I accepted. Working only 3 days a week would allow me to travel some week-ends and study others. It would be great. Dad didn't care which days I worked as long as I worked 3 days. I chose to work Tuesdays, Wednesdays and Thursdays. The only problem was that Dad was mostly using Homeopathy and Acupuncture to treat people and although he had treated me my whole life with Homeopathy, I really never studied it. So, I started studying Homeopathy and Acupuncture on week-ends.

Studying was something I knew how to do well. Homeopathy and Acupuncture were so fascinating to me. They were so different than conventional medicine. I had inherited Dad's passion for medicine and Mom's ability to listen to people's problems and understand them. The combination of skills was perfect for a medical practice. Within one year, the practice boomed and Dad and I were booked solid one month in advance. We had a lot of people on a waiting list.

I started looking for an apartment to rent. I didn't have much money so I rented a studio. Although it was small, I was thrilled that it was my own. I could decorate it exactly the way I wanted. My favorite colors were turquoise and purple. My favorite furniture was lacquered Chinese furniture. So, I furnished the apartment with beautiful custom made Chinese furniture and with all turquoise and purple carpets and paintings. The apartment was on the 5th floor of a building in town. It was bright and sunny with large windows and a Southern exposure. I loved the sun. I loved my first apartment. I was incredibly happy.

During my second year of private medical practice, I had more backaches. I had an X-ray taken which determined that my scoliosis was getting worse. In fact, it was steadily worsening by 1 degree angle each year. I needed surgery! I contacted the best scoliosis surgeon in Paris who said he could place a metal rod in my back to prevent the angle from getting worse. He could also take some bone from my hip and use it as a graft for my back to be stronger. I asked if he was performing any similar surgery in the next few weeks since I wanted to watch it before going under his knife myself. To my surprise, he said "Yes, as a matter of fact, I am doing the exact same surgery next week. You are welcome to be in the room but I am warning you, it is a difficult surgery to watch". I answered right away: "Thank you, I'll be there".

The following week, at 8:00AM, I was in the operating room, ready to watch the surgery which was supposed to start at 8:30. I didn't quite understand why any surgery could be difficult to watch. For me, surgery was surgery and I was always looking at it with cold uninvolved eyes. I didn't quite understand why the circulating nurse was asking me: "Are you sure, doctor, that you want to watch this surgery? Would you like to sit down? Are you feeling OK?" When they started bringing the patient in, I understood! The patient was a 20 year old young woman with a scoliosis similar to mine. The anesthesiologist put her under and as soon as she was sedated and intubated, 4 men started turning her around on her belly, attaching her neck and her pelvis to ropes. They then proceeded to pull her neck one way and her pelvis the other way as much as they could. That looked all too familiar to me and memories of when I was 11 years old came back to me. Then, with the patient's back fully extended, the surgeon made a large incision along her back and started using a hammer to dig in 2 vertebras in order to place a long rod in between the 2. The operating room looked like a torture room. The surgery was very bloody and very difficult to watch. Every half hour, a nurse would come to me to make sure I was okay and not going to faint - I kept reassuring her with a large smile: "no problem, everything is fine". This was not really true. I could easily have fainted. That's how hard it was to watch. At the end of the surgery, as my surgeon was taking his gloves and gown off, I went to him and told him: "I'll be next. Schedule me in 2 months".

2 months later, I was the patient on the operating table.

People would ask me: "why did you want to see the same surgery being done on someone else before?" Well, the answer is simple: I have seen so many different surgeons operating badly. I saw good surgeons taking their time, doing every cut perfectly. I saw bad surgeons, always stressed out and cutting in a hurry. Those are the ones that would make mistakes most of the time. I used to trust every doctor before medical school. Now, I don't have blind trust in every doctor anymore. I saw too many mistakes. I know too much about what is going on in hospitals, in operating rooms, in emergency rooms. This is why I wanted to see my surgeon operate. I wanted to make sure he wasn't one of those rushed and stressed out people. I wanted to make sure I could trust him. After watching him operate, I knew I could.

Some asked: "Why wait 2 months before having your surgery done?" Well, the answer is that I was very scared of the surgery. I thought I could end up being paralyzed. What if after surgery I couldn't move my feet any more? What if I died during surgery?

I wanted to live possibly the last 2 happy months of my life. I decided to fly to the United States and visit family members in New York and California. Flying to California was a dream I had for a long time. I didn't want to die without having visited California. So, I lived those 2 months as if they were the last 2 months of my life. I appreciated every second of my visit to Beverly Hills and Hollywood. I really fell in love with Los Angeles. It was hard to fly back.

Two days after my landing back in Paris, I was on the operating table, ready for the best but also prepared for the worse. I slowly lost consciousness as the anesthesiologist induced me.

When I woke up after surgery in my room, I was suffocating. I couldn't breathe! Something was pressing on my chest. I tried to breathe slowly and deeply but I couldn't. I realized that I was in a tight body cast. Tight it was, way too tight. I tried screaming but couldn't. I thought I was going to die. I started crying but it made my shortness of breath even worse. I then stayed there, breathing as shallow as possible to stay alive, hoping somebody would come. A nurse came in. She asked me if I was OK. I said "no, I cannot breathe, the cast is too tight". She said it was normal for the cast to be tight and she left. I felt hopeless and started crying again, just breathing shallow enough to stay alive.

It felt like several hours went by but it was probably only one hour when the door of my hospital room opened and to my relief my parents arrived. I was so happy. I knew Dad could help me. As he asked "how are you doing?", I answered "Dad, I cannot breathe, the cast is too tight, I have to breathe very shallow to stay alive, I told the nurse but she said it was normal and left, I feel I am going to die, I cannot inhale enough air" and I started crying.

Dad responded: "This is unacceptable!!! Don't worry; I'll take care of this". Dad was so wonderful; I knew I could count on him. He left the room quickly and 5 minutes later he was back with what seemed the whole hospital staff who paged my surgeon. He was here in no time, listened to my lungs, determined that the cast was indeed too tight and proceeded to cut it open in the chest area. Suddenly, I could breathe again!!! I was relieved.

Unfortunately, one hour later the anesthesia started to wear off and my back started to feel an intense pain. I had never experienced real prolonged physical pain before. Well, I caught up with that knowledge very quickly. The back pain was excruciating under the cast. That same pain lasted 4 weeks, day and night. Since no pain killer would relieve it, I stopped taking pain killers. No position would give me any relief. When I was lying on my back it was intense, when I was sitting it was intense, when I was standing up it was intense. I was miserable! I stayed in the hospital for 2 weeks then my parents took care of me at home. I'll always remember the way my mother was looking at me. It was so difficult for her to see me in so much pain! There was nothing she or my father could do to alleviate it. I just had to endure the pain and hopefully time would do its thing and little by little the pain would subside. I had to stay in my cast for 6 months. Fortunately, this time it was a washable one so I could take a shower with it.

During that very painful month, only one thought kept me in good spirits. I had done a beautiful 2 months trip before my surgery and I had done everything I wanted to do just in case I died. I was ready to die or to be crippled for life if such was my destiny. With that in mind, I waited for the pain to subside. Thank God, after 3 weeks, the pain started to decrease and after another 4 weeks I felt that I needed to have an activity to help me forget about the pain. I started to see patients again, even though I was wearing a body cast. None of my patients noticed anything or if they did, they didn't say anything. I had lost a lot of weight. I had no more fat on me. I was just a skeleton. With the cast on, it looked like I was my normal size. This is probably why nobody noticed anything. Seeing patients again helped my pain decrease even more. I could concentrate on my patients' problems rather than mine. That was a welcome change. As time went by, the pain started to go away. After 3 months, it was completely gone.

An interesting point here is that with a tight body cast, you cannot eat too much. I learned that very quickly. One day, I ate a large meal that dilated my stomach too much and the cast became so tight that I thought something inside of me was going to explode. It lasted a few hours. That meal taught me to not eat too much in order not to gain even a quarter pound. That turned out to be a great learning experience.

Six months went by quickly. It was soon time to cut my cast off. I didn't need it any more. I went to the hospital and the doctor cut it off. It felt so strange to be able to touch my body again. I felt so light, so light, so light … that I almost fainted. I couldn't get up. I couldn't stand up. My head was so dizzy. It felt like a part of my body was missing. It took me a few days to get used to being without my cast.

That is when I rediscovered a pure joy that everybody takes for granted. I could finally touch my body again. I could finally enjoy the pure delight of a hot bath. I was in heaven. People think that in order to be happy, they need a lot of money, they need to go to expensive, exotic places, they need expensive houses and cars. Well, I learned that all the money in the world doesn't necessarily bring happiness. Happiness is to be able to enjoy every single second of the pure joy of being alive. Happiness is being pain free, having lungs that breathe well, a heart that beats well, being able to walk, being able to be outdoors, hear the birds sing, smell the flowers, spend time with friends and family, and with the worst period behind me, being able to soak in a hot soothing bath. I had survived a difficult and painful surgery.

I was now well and the future was wide open for me with its endless possibilities. I didn't need more. I was fulfilled.

# Chapter 4
## "Chris, you should get married!"

The first 5 years of my private medical practice went by very fast. It was a very busy practice but I managed to take 2 months off each summer which allowed me to travel a lot. Once a year, I took an around-the-world plane trip with 6 to 8 stopovers in different countries. I visited the United States several times. I also visited Japan, Thailand, Korea and China.

After 5 years, Dad decided to retire. He sold his part of his medical practice to a very nice and competent physician, Dr. Lamothe. Dr. Lamothe and I worked well together and it was a pleasure sharing the same office.

My mother was always telling me: "Chris, you need to get married and have children. You don't want to be all alone at the end of your life. You need to find a husband!"

Well, I was not in a hurry to get married. Dating was a lot of fun but I knew I would soon be 30 years old… If I wanted to have children, this was the right time. This is when I met Martin. It was around Christmas time. I was skiing in the French Alps when I met this young man who fell in love with me. He was 3 years younger than me, good looking, tall, slim with beautiful brown eyes and brown hair. He was staying at the same Club Med as me. We had fun skiing together for one week. Then, when it was time to take the train back to Paris, he insisted on getting my phone number. I hesitated. I had a strong feeling that I shouldn't give him any information about me but I tried to be nice and at the end, I did give him my phone number in Paris. That was a mistake as I found out later. He started calling me regularly and we started dating. After 9 months of dating, he proposed. This should have been one of the happiest days in my life but somehow, it wasn't. In fact, I was very happy with him...in bed... and in bed only. He was a great lover and we would spend long week-ends in bed but as soon as we would get up, we couldn't get along. We were so different!!! That really worried me. I tried to talk to my parents about it. After all, they knew it all. They had life experience. They probably went through it themselves. In fact, they did. They told me: "You know, Chris, it was the same with us, as a matter of fact, when we got married, we barely knew each other but we still got married and as time went by, our love grew stronger and stronger. It will most likely be the same for you. If you like him, marry him and you'll see that love will grow stronger every day. Anyway, you will soon be 30 years old - it is time for you to settle down and have a family."

I wasn't sure I could live with Martin since I had never lived with a man before. Maybe my parents were right. After all they had experience and I had none. Of all the men I had dated, there was no other man I could possibly have married. So, why not try to marry Martin? It will be a great ceremony which I'll enjoy, and then, time will probably do its thing. So, I decided to accept. Martin was ecstatic!!!

Planning my wedding was wonderful! I bought the most beautiful dress, ordered the most beautiful flowers, and organized the most wonderful Catholic Church wedding and a big reception in a gorgeous restaurant.

All my patients were asking me about my progress in organizing the wedding. Half of the office visit time was telling my patients about all the details. They were as excited as I was.

Martin asked me if he could move in with me before the wedding and I said: "Absolutely not! It is a Catholic wedding and you can only move in after the wedding!" In fact, this was only part of the truth. The real truth, I couldn't tell it to anybody! The real truth is that I wasn't sure I could live with him. I was so happy living by myself and only seeing Martin on week-ends. That was absolutely perfect for me. I needed my privacy. I needed time by myself during the week, especially after putting in long hours at the office. I was actually dreading the moment when he would have to move in with me and I was trying to postpone it as much as possible. Unfortunately, I knew that I had to let him move in with me after the wedding. Once again, one week before the wedding, I expressed my fear to my parents. They immediately reassured me: "Don't worry; things will fall into place after the wedding". So, I didn't worry too much and focused completely on organizing the most beautiful and romantic wedding ever.

Finally, the day of the wedding arrived. I went to a hair stylist and had a gorgeous hair and make-up done. The church ceremony went marvelously well. It was so romantic! I was so beautiful in my white dress and Martin was so handsome in his tuxedo! As I said "I do", I was excited. It was the most wonderful day of my life. The reception was perfect and Martin and I went from table to table to talk to everybody. We had around 100 guests. I was the Princess and Martin was the Prince of the party. All our best friends, both our families and many of my patients were there. It was heavenly. We ate and danced until... early the following morning. Then everybody left, saying good night, thanking us and congratulating us. That is when we left Heaven! Martin and I went back to my apartment as Husband and Wife. We had a great night with great sex. Martin was so happy.

The following day Martin moved in with me, bringing all his furniture and belongings to my already crowded one bedroom apartment. That is when Hell started.

My first Wedding (30 years old)

Private medical practice in France

# Chapter 5
# The Disaster of Marriage

We had only been married for one week and I was already so tired. The only time I was happy with Martin was when we were in bed. There, he didn't rush things - we would spend hours and hours in bed, loving each other. Unfortunately, marriage consists of other things than being in bed. As soon as we were up, Martin had a fast pace. He walked fast, ate fast, expected me to do the same thing, expected me to cook, bake and clean fast like his mother, expecting me to wash his clothes and iron them as perfectly as his mother did. I, on the contrary enjoyed doing things slowly. I was not used to cooking or baking or ironing clothes. I had bought clothes for myself over the last 10 years that didn't need any ironing. I was a great doctor but a lousy housewife. When I came home from work, I was exhausted and I only wanted to rest. That was a bad beginning.

There was one way to save my marriage. I knew that Martin was applying for a new job. One of our common dreams was to live in Africa, Asia or the United States. It would be wonderful if Martin could get hired by a company that would need him in Africa, Asia or the United States. I would sell my medical practice and accompany him there. At the beginning, I would not work. I would learn to be a good housewife. Then I could start working again. That sounded like a great plan.

2 weeks later, Martin returned home from work with a large smile on his face. He just accepted his dream work. He was so happy. I asked him where the work was and if there was any travel involved. I held my

breath already dreaming about Africa…. He answered with a big smile: "It is in Paris and there is no travel involved but I couldn't refuse the position. It is with a new company. I am so excited". I almost fainted - "but Martin, what about a position abroad? I was so much looking forward to us working abroad!" He said he was sorry but that we would need to get used to staying in Paris. I felt my heart breaking. We had only been married 2 weeks and this was becoming a disaster. I started having horrible nightmares every night. I could hardly work during the day. I felt so sad all the time. I had no energy to do anything. I plunged into depression. I started to have a fever and sore throat. That's when a real disaster happened.

It was the weekend and we had been married for exactly 3 weeks. It was in January and it was cold outside. I was sick in bed with a fever. Martin thought that one of the water radiators in the apartment was not working. He decided to open it up to try to fix it. As he opened the large screw on top, suddenly water started gushing out of it. Hearing water running, I jumped out of bed and was horrified to see the entire apartment filling up with water very quickly. I screamed: "Martin, what did you do! Put the screw back!" Martin said "I am trying to but I cannot manage, I need to find the valve that stops the water in the whole apartment". He quickly left and I was alone with the raising waters. About 15 minutes later, the water stopped its gushing out of the radiator. Martin had managed to find the water valve and close it. When he returned, he put the screw back in the radiator valve and turned the water on again. The incident was over. Well yes, the incident was over but the disaster was still there. My entire apartment was soaked with water everywhere. That was it! I had enough! I was sick in bed with a fever, depressed, unhappy with my marriage, and the last thing I needed was a flooded apartment. This was too much. It was time to leave!

I called my parents, explained the situation and asked if I could stay at their house. Of course, my mother said yes. I packed a few things and 15 minutes later I was at my parents' house. I collapsed in tears in their arms explaining how unhappy I was in my marriage, how depressed I was and how sick I was. My mother put me to bed and I fell asleep.

When I woke up the following morning, my fever was still high. It remained high for an entire month. I had all kinds of tests to find out what type of bug I had. All tests came back normal. Unfortunately, the fever would not go down. My mood was very down too and I thought I was going to die.

In the past, patients had come to see me with similar symptoms. I would always tell them "your body is telling you something. You need to listen to it. What are you unhappy about? What do you want out of life? What were you born for? What is your dream?" I would push them to take a few steps towards their dreams. They would take my advice and little by little, with the help of acupuncture and homeopathy, they would get stronger and healthier. Some would change their life completely and would be transformed. From very depressed patients with a lot of backaches and stomachaches, they would metamorphose into beautiful, happy radiant, pain free human beings.

Now was the time for me to do the same thing. It was time for me to show myself the path to health and happiness – the way I had done for patients who were stuck in similar situations and didn't have the guts to get out. What did I really want in life? What was MY dream? Well, to answer this question truthfully, I really didn't want to be married at all at that time. Marriage felt like the end of my life. I did not want to live in Paris at all or elsewhere in France. My dream was to travel and perhaps work for Doctors Without Borders or Club Med in Africa, Asia or the United States. The limited travel I had done before my marriage was not enough. I wanted more – needed more. We didn't even go on a honeymoon! My other dream was to go to Los Angeles and do some acting there. I loved the Lee Strasberg's method of acting. I wanted to study it and perhaps be on TV or American movies. This marriage was clearly a mistake. I had to get an annulment in church and a divorce. After all, I had only been married 3 weeks!

My medical practice was going strong. I had more patients than I could possibly handle. I was booked solid one month ahead and had many people on the waiting list. I decided it was time to sell it. As I explained my decisions to my parents, I slowly started to feel better. They didn't argue. They could see that I was really miserable. They had never seen me like this before. They understood that it was time for me to move on.

After one month at my parents' house and only after I made the decision not to go back to Martin, my fever dropped. I had refused to see him until now but it was time for me to face him and tell the truth. I called him and asked him to come over my parents' house. In 10 minutes he was there in front of me. I realized I had no feelings for him. Seeing my husband of only 3 weeks didn't touch me a bit. My decision was made. "Martin, I said, I am so sorry but I made a mistake in marrying you. I want an annulment and a divorce. I need to live by myself. I am sorry." Martin was astonished. He tried to ask me why. He tried to understand and tried to get me to reconsider but there was nothing to understand and nothing to reconsider. I just couldn't live with him. I couldn't be his wife. I needed my freedom again.

Angry and sad at the same time, he left and went back to the apartment. I contacted a lawyer and filled out divorce papers.

# Chapter 6
# Freedom Again

It took one year for me to have an official divorce and to get an annulment from the church. During that year, I continued working in my private practice. When the divorce was finalized, I decided to sell the practice, sell my car and leave my apartment. I had been a private medical practice owner for 7 years. My patients were very attached to me and sad to see me leave. I was sad too but also very excited. I had an appointment with Doctors Without Borders the following week.

Doctors Without Borders! Those 3 words had always made me dream of dangerous and exotic medical missions. I had never been in a war zone and that was an experience I was wishing for. I wanted to experience war, battle fields and front zones. I had seen movies and heard war stories but living them was different. It was scary and exciting at the same time.

One week later, I was at Rue St Sabin in Paris at the Doctors Without Borders' headquarters. The person I had an appointment with was recruiting physicians. I was hoping there would be a mission for me as soon as possible. - I was ready for adventures! The recruiter was very nice and welcomed me very warmly. I felt comfortable immediately. "How soon would you like to work for us?" she said. I replied that I was available immediately. "Well, she said, we are looking for a physician to work in Mozambique, Africa in the town of Mocuba. This is in the north of the country which is a civil war zone. The physician hired will be in charge of an entire hospital for children. Would you be interested?" I could feel my heart pounding. Exciting thoughts raced through my mind. The mission was in a war zone. This was so awesome! This was exactly what I wanted. However, being responsible for an entire hospital for children was probably a bit too much for me since I was only a general physician and not a pediatrician. I was probably not qualified enough but I really wanted to accept. I would need to work on my pediatric knowledge in the next 10 days. The recruiter looked at me - waiting for my response. I heard myself saying "Yes, I would love to go but I am only a GP, I will need to study pediatrics a bit more". The recruiter seemed to be OK with that. She said "Can you leave in 10 days?" I answered yes with a big smile on my face. "I'll introduce you to all our people. We'll brief you with more details on your mission which requires a 6 months commitment. We'll provide you with all the shots you need and we'll help you learn Portuguese which is the language spoken in Mozambique." She got up and asked me to follow her.

She took me to a nurse who started giving me shots – first yellow fever, then hepatitis shot then on to Patrick who gave me more details on my mission: "Chris, you'll need to be careful. You will be in a civil war zone. Up North, in Mocuba where you'll be stationed, the hospital is safe but once or twice a week, you'll need to visit small towns around Mocuba to examine patients and determine who needs to be hospitalized. We'll fly you to those small towns and you'll fly the sickest patients back with you. You'll have a private plane and a private pilot – You won't be able to travel by road because all the roads are mined. The hospital you will be in charge of has 50 beds. There are a lot of very sick children suffering mostly from Kwashiorker which is a form of severe malnutrition with whole body swelling. There might be outbreaks of cholera. You'll need to be ready for those. As for malaria, it is endemic in Mozambique so we'll give you a mosquito net to sleep under. You'll do everything in Portuguese so you have 10 days to learn the language. Here is a book for you. You'll find in it all the main African diseases and the way to treat them. Good luck!"

When I left MSF which stands for Medecins Sans Frontieres which is the French term for Doctors Without Borders, I was high! I thought I was dreaming! I thought I was in paradise! They were sending me to a war zone! That was exactly what I wanted! I was going to be in charge of a pediatric hospital! What a huge responsibility! As far as Kwashiorker syndromes, I had never seen any nor had I seen any malaria cases. I had no idea how to speak Portuguese but I enjoyed learning foreign languages. Learning Latin in school turned out to be a major asset here. This would make Portuguese much easier to learn. The work would be on a voluntary basis. I knew I would not be paid. I already concluded that money cannot buy happiness. The year before, I was very wealthy and completely unhappy. Now I would be much poorer but also much happier. My happiness and fulfillment were priceless. They had to be priority number one from now on. I stopped by the bookstore "La Fnac" to buy the latest, most complete pediatric book and also tapes to learn how to speak Portuguese. I also bought a poster representing all the countries of the world.

The next 10 days went by fast. I learned everything I could about pediatrics, African diseases and the Portuguese language. I also learned about civil war. The Frelimo and Renamo were fiercely fighting against each other in Mozambique. The result was starvation for the people. Mozambique from 1891 to 1975 was known as Portuguese East Africa (a Portuguese colony) before acquiring independence from Portugal in 1975 thanks to the Frelimo. Frelimo stands for Frente de Libertacao de Mocambique – Mozambique Liberation Front. It was created in 1962 to fight against the Portuguese government. Renamo stands for Resistencia Nacional Mocambicana – Mozambican National Resistance. It was created in 1976 to fight against the Frelimo. Even though MSF was neutral, I would probably have to deal with Frelimo and Renamo people.

Finally, on April 1st 1990 at 7:00 am, it was time to get ready. I packed one large suitcase and one smaller bag. The large suitcase was very heavy but contained mostly books. I definitely brought more pounds of books than clothes. I proudly placed tags with MSF logos on each piece of luggage and hopped into Dad's car. My parents took me to the airport. They were very worried about me going to work in a civil war zone but at the same time they were very glad to see me happy and excited about life again. A brand new life awaited me.

The flight to Maputo, the capital of Mozambique, went fast. When I got off the plane, I was surprised to feel how hot the temperature was. My body loved that heat immediately. As I started looking around, I was astonished. I had never seen that many heavily armed men before. My heart started beating fast. I was entering a civil war country. It was very impressive. An MSF vehicle was waiting for me and took me to the MSF headquarters in Maputo. I met the first local MSF team and liked them immediately. I stayed overnight at their house and the following day, a small MSF plane flew me to Mocuba.

The hospital I worked at was a fairly modern one. It had a lab and X-Ray machine. I could routinely order blood tests. At all times, I had between 45 and 52 children hospitalized there. The Kwashiorker children were very impressive. They were so severely affected by malnutrition that their entire body was grossly swollen. Their faces, bellies, arms and legs were huge. They were so weak that they were prone to every disease. There were many cases of tuberculosis, leprosy and malaria. Every morning, I started doing rounds with the local nurses, examining each child and writing new prescriptions for medications and blood tests, all this in Portuguese of course. I started supervising the vaccination and the nutrition program for all the children around town. It was wonderful work. I felt I was doing so much for the children. It was very rewarding to see my little patients get stronger every day. I knew I made the right decision to work there after seeing their suffering faces evolve into delightful smiles.

The house I was living in was of a good size. I had someone to cook for me and wash my clothes. Life was good. I let my cook know that I wanted to adopt a pet. I always loved animals. I had always wanted to own a monkey and, since in Mozambique there were lots of monkeys, I thought our cook could find one for me. A few days later, he came to my room with a little funny foot-and-a-half foot tall monkey. I immediately fell in love with him. His face, hands and feet were all black, his belly was all white and his back was grey. I named him "Macacu" which means monkey in Portuguese. Macacu had a lot of energy and wanted to play all the time. He kept me very busy every night after work. He was a delight to be with.

Once a week, I would go to the local airport where my private pilot from South Africa would pick me up in his small twin engine plane and take me to one of the local dispensaries around in Gurue, Alto Molokue or Chinde. I especially liked Alto Molokue. It was in the mountains and the surroundings were beautiful! The air was so pure! I was forgetting that I was in a war zone. I would see a lot of patients there, adults and children and would fly the sickest ones back with me on my plane which was very small and had room for only 5 patients Once a month, I would take a day off to fly to the beach in Quelimane. There, I had to remember not to walk too far off tracks. Although there were no obvious signs of war, there could be bombs or mines buried in the sand.

After one month, I was very good at treating children and tropical diseases. I was also fluent in Portuguese and was starting to learn the local dialect. I had my routine well established and enjoyed it very much. I was so much happier there in the middle of Africa, doing voluntary work than my last year of private practice in France.

I loved flying days. I had the copilot seat. During my second month, Joe, my South African pilot started teaching me how to fly. Pretty soon, I was able to take off and fly most of the way. The views were breathtaking. The sensation of being in command of my plane was unforgettable.

Each flying day, I was invited to have lunch in the private house of the official leading the little town I was visiting. Lunch was a very pleasant break between clinics. The conversation was in Portuguese. It was customary for the leader to offer me the most delicious lunch he had to offer, which usually was a freshly killed roasted chicken. I thought I couldn't eat any chicken tastier than the French ones. Well, I was wrong. Those chickens in Mozambique were the best I had ever tasted. The owners had them running freely in their backyards all the time. They had no fat at all on them, only muscle. They were killed and roasted one hour before lunch. They were the best meals I had ever tasted. I can remember the way they tasted to this day.

One of my responsibilities was to visit shelters around the country to make sure that the people had enough flour, sugar and oil to survive. I would go from shelter to shelter asking when they last received flour, how much sugar they got and how much oil was left. Those food items were provided by several non profit organizations as well as MSF. That's when I learned about what I decided to call "evaporation". The first time, I was shocked then I got used to it. I had always thought that if the European Community was sending 20 tons of flour (we'll use flour as an example here) to the starving population of Mozambique, 20 tons of flour would be distributed evenly between all the starving people. That makes sense, right? Well, that was wrong. In reality, valuable things tend to "evaporate" along the way. The flour needs to get to Maputo airport, then it needs to be transported to the local towns. Several intermediary people need to intervene before the flour finally reaches the ones who need it the most. What I didn't know is that at each intermediary level, there would be a certain percentage of that flour that would "evaporate". Yes, the rich people would then get even richer (sell this extra "evaporated" flour) or give it to family and friends for them to enjoy or sell it. Finally and surprisingly, the real amount of flour that would practically get to the needy would be very small. Astonishing but true! That was one of my big revelations during my first mission.

Months went by fast. Soon, the end of my mission was approaching. I decided not to fly directly to France but to take one week of vacation in the nearby Zimbabwe to visit Harare, go to the Victoria Falls and then for a photo safari in the jungle. The first part of my trip was a real pleasure - I enjoyed the gorgeous waterfalls as well as the spectacular safari. The last part was a real disaster.

As I was in Harare, visiting the town, I walked through a main park. Being tired, I sat down on the lawn, putting my sweater on the grass and underneath my sweater hiding my handbag. All my important valuables were in my handbag, all my credit cards, cash, my passport, driver's license etc… On purpose, I hid it under my sweater so it would not to be a target for thieves which I knew could be numerous in Harare. 10 minutes into my rest, a group of 4 local young Zimbabwens approached me and started talking. They were very friendly. I talked to them for about 5 minutes and then, they left. Half an hour later, when I got up and looked for my handbag under my sweater, I couldn't find it. It was gone!!! That's when I understood what happened. While 3 of the men were distracting me with conversation, the 4th one had put his hand under my sweater to grab my handbag. When I finally realized what happened, I felt so stupid and angry. I should have known better! But it was too late. Everything was gone. I was horrified to discover the extent of the disaster. I had no more credit card, no more cash, no more passport, no more plane ticket. I had nothing left! Boy, did I feel stupid! I had to go to the police station to report the theft, then to the French embassy to get a temporary passport.

The French embassy did a great job and managed to fly me back to Paris. I sighed with relief when my plane landed in Charles de Gaulle airport, France. I took the RER to go back home and with pleasure, I found my parents waiting for me. It was so wonderful to be back home after my mission in Mozambique and my disastrous trip to Zimbabwe. I had so much to talk about that we stayed up very late that night. The following day, I was at the MSF headquarters in Paris for my debriefing. Altogether, it had been a very positive mission and I was proud of my accomplishments on behalf of MSF. The recruiter from MSF asked me when I would be available for another mission. I said I wasn't quite ready yet but I would call as soon as I was. I left MSF headquarters feeling very light and happy. I had successfully achieved my first MSF mission. I was now on vacation and the whole world was open to me. The weather outside was beautiful and sunny. The sky was blue. I started walking along the streets of Paris, just enjoying being in the Moment.

It took one week for me to de-stress and relax. After one week, I was ready for more adventures. I wasn't ready to work for MSF again just yet. I had heard that Club Med was hiring physicians for some of their vacation resorts. I was curious to see if they could hire me for some exotic destination. I contacted the Club Med recruiter who told me to drop by her office with a resume. I did that immediately. The lady was very nice and we became friends right away. She said she needed someone urgently to work for one week in a Club Med in Spain. She couldn't find any physician available to leave tomorrow and was wondering if I would be willing to do it. I accepted right away and the following day I was in Marbella, Spain as the Club Med physician. That particular Club Med had a lot of children and needed a physician to examine the children that were sick. It was a pleasant job and the week went by fast.

10 days later, I was back in Paris in the Club Med recruiter's office. She was very happy I had been able to accommodate her and since everyone in Marbella was happy with my work, she offered to fly me to the Ivory Coast and work at the Assinie Club Med for 6 months. It was a longer contract and a special deal. Here was the deal: I would be the Club Med physician but I would also be a GO (in French it stands for "Gentil Organisateur") which means I was required to participate in the evening shows (which are organized for the GM which stands for "Gentil Membre"). When I heard this, I jumped with excitement. This would be so wonderful. It would allow me to fulfill my 2 passions in life. The first one was medicine; the second one was show business. At Club Med, I could be an actress performing on stage at night and a physician during the day. I couldn't wish for anything better. I accepted immediately and one week later in October 1990, I was on a plane for the Ivory Coast. One thing I didn't mention was the pay. It was really close to nothing, however, I would have virtually no expenses since I would have a guest bedroom at the resort and would be fed everyday just like the tourists. If I had time I could do all the touristy activities offered by the resort for free. I was thrilled.

I arrived with the tourists in Abidjan. A large van took us to the Assinie resort where all the GO's welcomed us with music and dances. This was starting to be fun. When I mentioned that I was the GO physician, the chief of the village came to personally welcome me. I was taken to my room, then to a beautiful buffet dinner. After dinner, I was taken to my office near the infirmary and introduced to my 2 nurses. They were young and beautiful as were all the GOs. I felt immediately at ease with them and I felt immediately at home in Ivory Coast.

Then, my wonderful routine started. I only needed to be in my office 1 hour in the morning and 2 hours at night. The rest of the time, I had to be on call 24 hours a day but I was rarely called. The main problems were malaria and bronchitis for the GO's. As for the GM (the tourists), their main problems were traumas. They would hurt themselves during waterskiing, volleyball or tennis. Others would catch colds, while others would get sunburns or indigestion from eating too much. The medical problems were very simple and easy to address. When I wasn't in the office, I was waterskiing, sailing, kayaking or swimming. Not a bad life at all! Breakfasts, lunches and dinners were all buffets and they were incredibly delicious. The Assinie Club Med had several chefs on staff full time plus a baker specialized in breads and a patisserie specialist baking the most incredible cakes. Every day the menus would change. I remember to this day how delicious all the meals were. I was especially fond of all the various grilled fish and the deep fried vegetable bananas. As for the freshly baked chocolate cakes, strawberry and raspberry mousses, I had never tasted any thing like them. For breakfast, we had freshly squeezed papaya juice, mango juice, pineapple juice and many more. It was heavenly.

The weather was hot and humid the way I loved it. All the rooms were air conditioned but I rarely needed to use it. I just loved African weather. My body definitely preferred living in Africa than living in France where I was always too cold.

In the evenings, we would rehearse dances for the following week's shows. Almost every evening I managed to be on stage. I was in almost every show and I loved it. During the day, I was this serious physician dealing with life and death situations while at night I would metamorphose into a sexy dancer. The first 3 months, I was still reserved then, I let go of being reserved and became extremely provocative on stage. Tourists would love it and I would receive a lot of applause. The following day, tourists would line up at my office to talk to me. I became very popular. Those 6 months ended up being some of the best months of my life because my 2 passions were expressed equally. I was blossoming.

Six months went by very fast and pretty soon I found myself packing to catch the next plane to Paris. The experience had been unforgettable. Twelve hours later, I was on the RER again heading towards Bourg-La-Reine.

After one week in Paris, I was ready to leave again. This time I was ready for another MSF mission again. I had eaten all the food I could eat for 6 months and was ready for more difficult conditions. I decided to spend the next few years alternating between MSF assignments and Club Med contracts. I liked the drastic contrast between the two. The differences were fascinating. At Club Med, I was treating rich tourists who were overeating, drinking too much alcohol, smoking too much and had traumas while playing. At MSF, I was treating extremely poor people in refugee camps who were suffering from starvation, struggling to find enough fresh drinkable water to survive every day, struggling to get enough flour, sugar and oil to feed their family. The contrast was amazing.

I decided I would visit Doctors Without Borders's headquarters the following day. It was so exciting! Would they have a new mission for me? How soon? Where? It could be anywhere in the world; it could be in a war zone or a natural disaster zone. I went to my bathroom and looked at the large poster I had put on my bathroom wall. It was a world poster. It was so exhilarating to have the whole world exposed in front of me like this. Anything could be possible. Tomorrow, I would know where my new assignment would be. I could hardly wait. I needed excitement in my life. I was curious to go to another war zone. Life here in Paris was just too boring. I could hardly fall asleep that night.

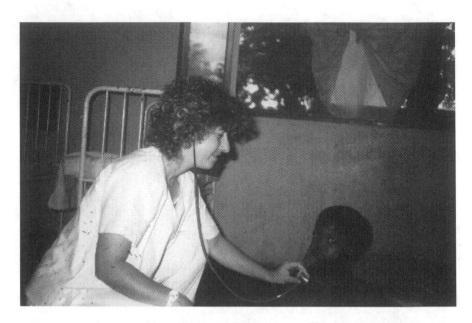

Mocuba Hospital in Mozambique

My monkey and I in Mozambique

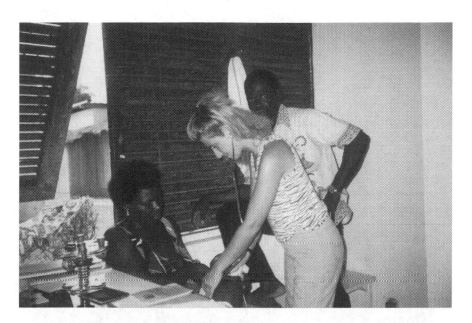

Working in Ivory Coast

Club Med show dancing the French Cancan

# Chapter 7
# War Zone

*April 1991*

The following day, I took the metro to go to the Doctors Without Borders' headquarters and met the person in charge of the assignments.

She said: "Your last mission in Mozambique went well. Are you ready for a second mission?"

"Yes, I am" I said. I could hardly wait to hear where I would be needed.

"Well" she added "we need somebody to replace a physician who is completely burned out in Madhu refugee camp. This is a 27,000 people refugee camp in the North of Sri Lanka. Madhu is a sacred area in Tamil territory controlled by Tamil Tigers. We are in good terms with the army and with the tigers at this time but they are fighting each other in a civil war. We are neutral. If you accept this mission, you will have to leave as soon as possible. You will first fly into Colombo which is full of tourists, then, you'll be transferred to the North of the Island which is in the civil war area and closed to tourists. Would you accept to go there and if so, how soon can you leave?"

"This is exciting!", I thought to myself, "going to Sri Lanka, where I have never been, first to Colombo and then to a civil war zone! Wonderful!"

I accepted right away and said I would be ready to go in a couple of days. The recruiter was thrilled and said she would contact the current physician to let her know the good news. She had finally found a replacement for her. She will finally be able to rest.

I went back home very excited, told my parents all about my future mission, spent 10 minutes in my bathroom, looking at my world poster and started studying the history of the island.

Sri Lanka was an island located 18 miles off the Southern Coast of India. It was famous for its production and export of tea, coffee, rubber, cinnamon and coconuts. It was a multi-religious, multi-ethnic nation with Sinhalese people forming the majority of the population (74%) while Sri Lankan Tamils mostly concentrated in the Northeast were forming the 2nd largest community. Sri Lanka had been a British Colony until 1948 when it became independent. Since 1983, there was a very bloody civil war between the Sinhalese dominated government and Tamil insurgents demanding an independent Tamil state in Northeastern Sri Lanka.

After the whole evening talking to my parents about my future mission, we determined that it would be a very easy one and probably not a dangerous one. The future proved us all wrong...

The flight to the largest town of Sri Lanka - Colombo was very pleasurable and it was great to arrive in a touristic area. As I got off the plane, I was shocked to feel how hot it was. I usually love hot weather. I am a real "lizard". The hotter the better; but this was really hot, barely tolerable for me. After I picked up my luggage, I saw a man holding a large sign above his head. The sign said "Doctors Without Borders". I went straight to him. He said "Are you doctor Chris Gilbert?" I said yes. His face lightened up and with a great big smile showing beautiful white teeth on a very dark face, he said "Welcome to Colombo". He then grabbed my luggage and took me to his car. One hour later we stopped in front of 24/4 Guildford Crescent. I recognized the MSF logo. I was "home".

The house was big with a lot of rooms. In most of the rooms were two or 3 beds. I was taken to a room with 3 beds. Only one of the beds was not occupied. I put my suitcase on it then proceeded to the bathroom to freshen up. It was hot! I then went downstairs where I met the local chief of the mission, Henry. He said: We'll try to get you on your way to Anuradhapura tomorrow and then Madhu the day after tomorrow. In Anuradhapura, Isabelle, one of your nurses from Madhu will meet you and will take you to Madhu. Sylvie, the physician you are replacing is very tired and she needs some rest. The sooner we get you there, the better it will be. In the meantime, dinner is ready! Let's go eat!"

I followed Henry to the dining room where a large table was set up with around 10 people sitting there already. He introduced me to everybody. Everybody was very nice and dinner was simply delicious. This was my first contact with Sri Lankan food and I loved it immediately. After a hot night, at 6:00am the following day, I was ready to go. The same chauffeur that picked me up at the airport was there. He smiled at me with a great "good morning doctor", put my luggage in the trunk and opened the door for me. It was the beginning of a great adventure. A few hours later, we arrived in Anuradhapura. We went to a beautiful colonial style hotel. This is where I met Isabelle for the first time. She was a little younger than me, from Paris too, very nice and cute. She had been working in Madhu for 3 months and had just come to Anuradhapura to pick me up and start telling me about my new work. She said there were a lot of sick people in Madhu refugee camp and Sylvie was the only physician there, on call 24/7. We needed to get there as soon as possible. I couldn't agree more. It was great to finally meet somebody I would be working with on an everyday basis. I immediately felt comfortable with Isabelle. Since it was getting late, we spent the night in this hotel and had a great dinner. It was the last tourist town before entering the war zone. The hotel was very big with a great colonial rich architecture. We were the only ones for dinner and probably the only ones in the hotel. Our rooms were big and very comfortable. I slept well that night, happy to be in Sri Lanka.

The following day, at 6:00am, we checked out of the hotel and our chauffeur took us to Vavuniya which was at the border of the war zone.

There, men from the Sinhalese army stopped us. They were heavily armed. They told us we couldn't go any further. Isabelle started talking to them to convince them to let us go further north. They still refused. After one hour of pleading, they finally accepted. We quickly got back to our car and went on our way thinking they might change their mind if we weren't fast enough.

We were entering the civil war zone! I was thrilled. My eyes were wide open! After 2 hours of driving, we saw people running. They were local people running away from where we were going. The more we drove, the more people we saw running the opposite direction. This didn't look good! That's when I saw the first Tamil Tigers. They were 10 then 20 then at least one hundred. They were not walking the same direction as the other people. They were going the same direction as us. Most of them were very young. I looked closely and was astonished: They were children! Heavily armed! 8 to 17 years old! They looked nice, looking at our vehicle and smiling at us. They looked so young and innocent! We were overtaking them quickly. That is when I got really worried! Something didn't look right! I had a strange bad premonition.

As we continued advancing, suddenly, there was nobody else on the road. Then one mile further, we were stopped by heavily armed men. I looked more closely. My God, this was the Sinhalese army! But didn't we just see more than one hundred Tamil Tigers heading our way? I got really scared. The army refused to let us go any further. They looked like very nice people, young also, smiling easily. We tried to plead but it was useless. During the time Isabelle was pleading with them, I was constantly looking back. The Tamil Tigers were for sure going to arrive soon and we might be in between the 2. We had to get out of the danger zone! Isabelle turned around to tell me: "We have to go back to Vavuniya! They are refusing to let us go any further". I told her that it was fine with me but that we had to hurry. The Tamil Tigers would be here soon. We hopped back in our vehicle and turned around. After 5 minutes on our way back, our driver stopped and told us to get out of the vehicle. I couldn't understand why. Suddenly I saw a quarter mile ahead of us about one hundred Tigers. They had their guns and bazookas in their hands and were aiming at us. They had stopped and more and more Tigers were arriving behind them and joining them. Our driver gave us a white flag and an MSF flag and told us to start walking towards them. He was going to follow us driving our vehicle. We did what he said. As I started walking slowly towards the Tamil Tigers who had us at gunpoint, I wasn't scared any more. I recognized the children who were smiling at us an hour ago. As we came closer, they recognized us too and stopped pointing their guns at us. They smiled at us again. They were so young and beautiful.

After we passed them, we went back in our vehicle and started heading towards Vavuniya again. 15 minutes later, we heard gun shots, so many gun shots, so many gun shots… Tears came down my eyes. I couldn't stop those tears, thinking that the kids I just saw, the ones that were smiling at us were killing and being killed. They were fighting the army which was made of young men equally nice and friendly. I had never been on a war front before. To walk from the army who were smiling at us to the Tigers who were also smiling at us, leave and then hear 15 minutes later that they are shooting at each other was TERRIBLE!

We, MSF, were neutral; we had friendly relationships with the army and also with the tigers. Our goal was to protect the population, women and children who were defenseless. I had to stay calm. We drove back to Vavuniya where we tried to see the army Major in Chief. He was a very nice man. He explained that the fighting was too harsh West of Vavuniya. It was too dangerous for us to go through. We slept in Vavuniya that evening, hoping to go through the following day. Unfortunately, the following morning, we were told that the fights had intensified. "The situation might remain bad for a few days" the Major in Chief said. This is when we contacted Henry again who told us to drive back to Colombo.

I had mixed feelings about driving back to Colombo. My first reaction was to be disappointed not to be in Madhu yet and sad for Sylvie who wouldn't get the relief she expected. My other reaction was to be very happy: I'll have time to play tourist and explore the capital Colombo.

As we arrived at the MSF house again, I settled in the same bedroom as I was 3 nights prior; then, I changed clothes and explored Colombo. I did a lot of shopping, bought two beautiful rings: a 22 carat gold one and an amethyst one. I was happy. Yes, I was a doctor on a medical mission but I was also a woman who loved shopping and jewelry. As I came back to the MSF house for a great Sri Lankan dinner, Henry told me I was invited to go to Negombo for the week-end. That week-end was the special "MSF-Negombo week-end" where all the MSF teams from the Island were gathering to discuss all the issues. I was really lucky to be able to attend. This kind of week-end was only held once every 3 months. Sylvie was the one who was supposed to attend after the end of her mission. Unfortunately she was still working 24/7 in Madhu.

As we were driving to Negombo, I looked at the beautiful countryside. Negombo was at the seaside, one hour North of Colombo. It was a great tourist town with luxurious hotels. The one we stayed at had delicious buffets, swimming pool and water ski on a Laguna. We were 20 MSF people to attend the conference. It was very interesting to have an overview of all the goals MSF was trying to achieve in the different parts of the island including in Madhu. The weather was fantastic, food was delicious, and I was in paradise.

Our last evening in Negombo, as we were having dinner, I saw a man in his 40's eating by himself at a table next to ours. He looked very nice. I started talking to him. I was curious to find out who he was. Was he a tourist or a physician on a mission for another organization? It turned out he was a Norwegian diplomat, based in Colombo. His name was Lars. As we continued talking, I offered him to sit at our table which he gladly did. He was 15 years older than me and very attractive. He was at the age when rested, he looked young, but tired, he looked old. It was, as I called it, the in between age. He was blond with beautiful blue eyes, tall, slim, very handsome…and married…His wife was in Norway… There was an instant bond between us. That night, he was going back to his house in Colombo. He invited me for dinner the following evening in Colombo since we were scheduled to drive back too. I accepted.

That Sunday night, Lars invited me to eat Chinese food in Colombo. Yes, there was a Chinese restaurant in Sri Lanka. You will tell me, what a waste! Why not eat Sri Lankan food? Well, you see, I love Chinese food and I figured that since I was going to be in Sri Lanka for 6 months, I would have plenty of Sri Lankan meals. Chinese meals on the other hand… this could be my last one in 6 months. Lars offered me to play table tennis before dinner at his house. I was thrilled. He picked me up at the MSF house and took me to his house which was huge, luxurious and had a colonial style. He had some local personnel working for him. One person was preparing his food while another one was taking care of the house cleaning. It was another type of life, a diplomatic type of life which I loved right away. We had a great time playing table tennis. I could have stayed there forever. It was so comfortable and easy to be with Lars. I was starting to fall in love. It seemed that we had the same habits and the same taste for a lot of things. It was so strange to find a man I was instantaneously so close to here in Sri Lanka as I was about to leave again the following morning for another attempt to go to Madhu. Late that evening, we went to the Chinese restaurant. It was in a very luxurious hotel for tourists and food was delicious. Then, he took me back to the MSF house. It broke my heart to have to say goodbye to him. I didn't know when or if I could see him again. I didn't know when or if I would be in Colombo again. All I knew is that I was scheduled to leave again the following morning early Monday to try to go to Madhu. We decided to stay in touch by radio contact. We would talk every night at 9:00pm.

I slept well that night; I had sweet dreams of love. At 5:00am, my alarm clock brought me back to reality. It was time to get up and hit the road up north again. We loaded our MSF vehicle again and our chauffeur drove us north to Anuradhapura. It was a new chauffeur and he got a bit lost. We ended up in Kandy, very charming little town in the mountain. Finally, I knew where Kandy sugar was coming from… from sugar cane coming from Kandy. I had my eyes wide open to look at the houses and the countryside of Kandy. We then headed to Vavuniya where the army told us again that we couldn't go any further. Déjà vu! This time the major looked really embarrassed and told us he would organize a helicopter transfer for us to Mannar at the extreme north of the island the following day. From Mannar, it would be easier for us to get to Madhu. We accepted. We went to our favorite hotel in Anuradhapura to spend the night. I had now been in Sri Lanka 9 days and still didn't know my future work place…

That night, I wrote a letter to my parents telling them about all the difficulties to get to Madhu. I especially told them not to worry: "Mom and Dad don't worry" I wrote "nobody can attack us. If somebody does, either a soldier from the army or a Tamil tiger, it is an international scandal. Consequently, we are extremely safe. We are completely neutral. We are bringing medications for the population and both the army and the Tamil people appreciate our help a lot. We couldn't be any safer". Little did I know how unsafe we were. It was only my second mission in civil war zone and I was still very naïve and young.

The following day, as soon as I got up, I heard that the helicopter trip to Mannar had been cancelled. In the same hotel, were staying people from the United Nations having for mission to bring food to the refugees. They had 11 trucks full of food items (flour, sugar, dry milk) and were on their way to Madhu. We asked them if they could take us. They said "with pleasure". 2 hours later we were in one of the 11 united nations' trucks, on our way to Madhu.

The road was in very bad shape and we had to go very slowly to avoid large holes. It took forever to get to Madhu but finally, after 5 hours, we got there. I was finally at the place where I would work for 6 months. As I got out of the truck, I saw a Caucasian thin brunette running towards me. That was Sylvie, the physician I was replacing. She was so happy to see me. She would be able to go back to Paris soon after a debriefing in Colombo and I would take over her work. There was a lot to be done.

As we headed towards the MSF house, I was struck by how hot it was outside. It was over 100 degrees F. The house was small and very hot inside. It was 90 degrees in the bedrooms and there was no electricity which means no fan, no air conditioning, no light, and no hot water. All those things that you take for granted didn't exist there. She took me to my room which I was going to share with my 2 nurses. It was a small room with 3 beds and mosquito nets around each one. There was malaria here and we had to be protected. Then, she took me to the "hospital" which was a concrete small building with space for only 5 beds. It would have to be expanded so that we could hospitalize more people.

Then, we went to the refugee camp where 27,105 people were under tents provided by the United Nations. I was struck by the beauty of the people. Women and men were tall, thin with very dark skin and very delicate face features. Their eyes were beautiful, large, dark expressing deep sensitivity and strong intelligence. They were also expressing a lot of suffering. Their smiles were beautiful. They had that unique way of saying yes: They would say yes while shaking their head from side to side. The very first time, I got confused because shaking my head from side to side means no for me. But for them, it means yes. After a few days, I got used to it and I found their shaking their head very cute.

Then, we went to the MSF vehicle were Sylvie showed me how to do radio contacts with Colombo. I had to do a radio contact 3 times a day, once in the morning, once at lunch time and once in the evening. We were indeed isolated here. She then showed me our medication supply, food supply, water supply and the place where we were examining patients everyday. She was running short of medications before we arrived but fortunately, we brought a lot of them. Then, she packed and she left me in charge.

Suddenly, I was chief on board. I had 2 MSF French nurses and several Sri Lankan helpers working with me but I was the only physician! What a huge responsibility! My routine started. I had to wake up early to do my first radio contact with Colombo at 7:00 am then I had to walk to the hospital for regular clinics every morning from 8:00 am to 12:30 pm. There were a lot of wild dogs fighting along the way. I was hoping they didn't have rabies. I would see patients the whole morning. Mornings were good to work because the temperature was still bearable. Then, in the afternoon, it was much hotter and less bearable. I was doing prenatal clinics from 3:00 pm to 6:30 pm every day except Thursdays when I was doing postnatal clinics. I was on call the rest of the day and every night. Patients had mostly upper and lower respiratory tract infections, malaria, bloody and non bloody diarrhea, conjunctivitis and asthma. They were easy to treat. Snake bites, fox and dog bites were more difficult to treat. I had to hospitalize about 25 persons per month. Very often, I was woken up in the middle of the night. One night, at 2:00am, a woman frantically knocked on our door. She was carrying a dying child in her arms. He had severe diarrhea and was severely dehydrated. He needed IV fluids. We walked him to the hospital in the middle of the night (with a large wooden stick in our hands because there were a lot of wild dogs in the streets) and tried to start an IV drip. Unfortunately, the child was so dehydrated that we couldn't find any accessible vein. He died 10 minutes later. We were not able to revive him.

Another time at 1:00am, a man violently banged on our door. His face was bleeding heavily with half of his Right cheek hanging out. He had just been attacked and bit by a wild dog! I spent a large part of the night at the hospital taking care of him. Another night, a man came because of a scorpion bite on his foot. There were indeed scorpions here and since most people were bare feet, scorpion bites were always a risk.

Our vaccinations program went well until our solar refrigerator died. I had to stop all vaccinations for a month until we got it repaired. I also had to supervise the feeding center we created for children and the construction of latrines. We had 250 latrines! That was not enough for 27,105 persons. We needed 300 more!

I had to supervise the chlorination of water reservoirs. One kilogram of chloride per day was placed in each tank which was not enough. I had to change this to one and a half kilogram per day. 80 water taps were open and 130 more were ready to be open soon. As for dogs, the Sri Lankan officials started killing all the wild dogs which made the camp more secure.

In the month of April 1991, we saw 5,200 patients in regular clinic, did 450 consults in prenatal clinics, examined 291 pregnant women and delivered 82 babies. We had 35 deaths. Among those, 24 were from old age, 3 were children who died from acute diarrhea, 4 were children who died from malaria, one from encephalitis, one from meningitis and 2 from unknown cause.

My personal life was simple. I loved my evenings there. I made my last radio contact with Colombo at 8:00 pm then I went to our bathroom and washed up with my usual bucket of water. Yes, a bucket of water that I would fill up several times and pour over my body because we had no shower and no hot water. We only had a large container of water by a sort of bathtub in which we would dip our little bucket as needed. I went to bed early since we had no electricity and read in bed with a candle light under my mosquito net. At 9:00 pm, I would get up again to make my secret radio contact with Lars. He was doing well and was worried about me. The war situation was getting worse in the north of the island but everything was good in Colombo and he was thinking about me a lot. Then, back in bed, I would blow my candle off and would fan myself to sleep. It was between 87 and 95 degrees in the bedroom at night!

Next door to our house were people working for the United Nations. They had a real shower with cold water. I made friends with them and once a month, I would ask them if I could use their shower. Do you know how good a real shower feels (even with cold water) after a month of washing with a bucket? It feels heavenly! We forget about all the things we take for granted.

As days went by, I started being woken up at night, not by sick patients but by the sounds of bombings. Bombings around Madhu were intensifying as Lars was saying. Very soon, I heard bombings every day, day and night. They were all around us, mostly North, East and South of us. I went to bed hearing them, woke up hearing them, and I examined patients hearing them. I reported this in my daily radio contacts. I didn't think much of this. I was young and untouchable. I knew I was in a sacred place, Madhu. I knew nobody would touch Madhu. I was safe. I didn't even get scared until…

It was my turn to get a week of rest in Colombo. I was so looking forward to see Lars again. Each of the people from our team was getting a week off every 2 months. Those 2 months had gone by so fast! Radio contact with Colombo 3 times a day, seeing patients at the clinic everyday, having from 1 to 4 hospitalized patients to take care of and being on call 24/7 will do that to you. It will make time go by very fast. So, finally, it was my turn to go to Colombo. We had one physician Ob-Gyn and his wife, a nurse who had just come to spend a month with us. They had to go back to Colombo and then Paris. Since one of our drivers had to take them back to Colombo, I decided to go with them. The evening before, I had a great talk on the radio with Lars. We were planning on playing tennis, golf and table tennis together. I was also very much looking forward to taking a hot bath. Just the thought of it was making my whole body shiver with pleasure of anticipation.

That morning of my departure for Colombo, as I was finishing packing, my nurse Patricia, came to me. She was very tired and very depressed. She needed a break very badly. I really wasn't very tired and I was not depressed at all. I was in much better shape than her! She was the one that really needed to go to Colombo, not me. It only took me a few seconds to think it over. I was the team leader here. I was the one that was responsible for my nurses and for their well being. I could not go to Colombo, have fun and leave Patricia working here. I decided to have her take my place and go to Colombo instead of me. Her eyes were so sad but suddenly, they sparkled with hope as I told her my decision: "Really, Chris, are you sure? What about you, your break and your Norwegian diplomat?" I told her I would go on a break a month later, no big deal. She came to me and hugged me with joy. "Thank you so much, Chris! You won't regret it!" Ironic words, when you know the future…

A few minutes later, she had gathered all her clothes, probably afraid I was going to change my mind. Half an hour later, I was seeing her, our visitor Ob-Gyn, his wife and our driver off toward East. Patricia sat on the front seat. I waved at her. She had a big smile on her face.

I proceeded to unpack and get ready to go to clinic. As I was about to leave, about 45 minutes after Patricia had left, I heard bombing starting again. They seemed so close and were coming from East. I went to the car and turned on the radio for an additional radio contact to Colombo. That's when I heard….

It was Patricia's voice: "Colombo or Madhu or anybody else, please answer me, we are bombarded by the army, please somebody answer, please somebody stop this! Help! Help!" I answered quickly. "Patricia, this is Chris, what is happening?"

Patricia: "2 helicopters from the army are over us and are shooting at us. There is a plane coming towards us, oh, Chris I am so scared, it is… oh, no, it is bombarding.

Me: "Stay calm, Patricia, we have a big sign on the roof of our car that says we are Doctors Without Borders. The army should recognize our vehicle and not attack us. I'll try to contact Colombo. Colombo! Colombo! Are you there? Colombo, Colombo, this is an emergency, Colombo, Colombo!!"

I knew we had a white flag in the vehicle. MSF's recommendations in case anything like this would happen, was to grab this flag, get out of the vehicle and wave it at whoever was attacking us. Was that the right thing to do? I was wondering. It could be dangerous too.

Nobody in Colombo was answering. This was not a usual time for our communications. I knew how the radio was set up in Colombo. It was in the main office. Their radio was on at all times but there was somebody close to it only part of the time. Our radio transmission was set to be 3 times a day but in between, there was not automatically somebody there in the office and right now, nobody was answering. I was the only one on the air. I could hear planes and shootings coming from East. They sounded so close. Patricia's vehicle was not far away from here. I started shivering. The army should really not attack us. Our Doctors Without Borders sign is painted on the roof of all our vehicles. It is so big. It is so easy to see it and recognize it from the air! Why are they attacking us? I couldn't understand. I had to think fast. Patricia was panicking. I was the only one on the radio to help her. I decided to stick with the Doctors without borders guidelines.

Me: "Patricia, our guidelines are to grab the white flag, get out of the car and waive it at the people attacking. Can you find the flag?"

Patricia: "Yes, here it is. I found it. Chris I am so scared! Oh, my god, they are coming back!"

Me: "Patricia, get out of the car and waive the flag!"

Patricia: "O.K."

I heard more shootings and bombings. Then silence.

Me: "Patricia, are you O.K.? Can you hear me?"

No answer.

10 minutes later, Patricia's voice:

Patricia crying: "Chris, I am bleeding, Chris, please, come and save me. Chris, I got out of the car and I waived the white flag but they still shot at me. I got shot in the leg. It hurts so much and I am bleeding so much. Oh, my god, they are coming back, I need to run."

I heard more shooting and bombings. Nobody came on the radio anymore.

I had to think fast. Patricia's vehicle was not far away, maybe only 20 miles away. I should take my vehicle to get her. But no, it would be too dangerous and my vehicle too could get attacked. I had to find a way to contact Colombo. They had to intervene. But what about Patricia, how badly was she injured? She needed help and medical care as soon as possible. I tried calling Colombo again.

"Colombo, Colombo, anybody there?"

After what seemed to be an eternity but in reality was only a few minutes, I heard: "This is Henry in Colombo"

Me: "Henry, we need your help, Patricia just got injured" I explained the whole story, offering to go and get Patricia since she was probably very close by.

Henry: "You need to stay in Madhu. It would be too dangerous for you to leave. I am going to contact the army right now and ask for a cease-fire. I'll organize everything to get her and bring her back to Colombo. Stay where you are. I am taking care of everything!"

I was relieved. I knew Henry would do the right thing. I waited a little by the radio listening to Henry trying to contact Patricia's vehicle but nobody answered. I could hear the fighting and bombings going on. I could only hope that Patricia was still alive. I could only hope that our Ob-Gyn, his wife and our driver were not injured. I went back to clinic that day, still thinking about Patricia. A particular thought was very present in my mind: I was the one that should have been in the vehicle. I was the one that was meant to travel to Colombo that day…

During clinics, I had one ear on my stethoscope and the other one listening to bombing sounds. After 2 hours of clinic, all bombings stopped around Madhu. I sighed with relief. MSF had probably managed to get a cease-fire. Hopefully, Patricia will be saved.

As I came back to the house after clinic, I heard gun shots and bombings again. I did my usual radio contact with Colombo, eager to hear if Patricia had been saved. What I heard came as a huge shock.

Henry: "We managed to have the army cease fire for a few hours and got Patricia. She is very badly wounded in her leg. The Ob-Gyn is only slightly injured. His wife is fine. As for your driver, he is slightly injured too. Patricia is currently in a hospital in Colombo and will be transferred to France as soon as she is in stable condition. We, Doctors Without Borders, have decided to pull out of Sri Lanka. It is getting too dangerous for us. We'll get you out of Madhu as soon as possible but right now, the roads are not safe enough. We won't be able to send you any more medical supplies since we are stopping all operations. Keep on doing your work as usual and we'll organize your safe departure. We'll contact your family to reassure them. This is making headline news all over the world. Hang in there."

I was astonished! MSF was pulling out of Sri Lanka? I was happy that Patricia had been found alive and was well taken care of, but that Doctors Without Borders would get out of Sri Lanka over this completely astonished me. What about the 27,000 people I was taking care of? Who would take care of them? We just couldn't abandon them?

The next 2 weeks went very fast. MSF Colombo was trying to get me out of Madhu but fighting had intensified again, roads were mined and it was too dangerous to fly. I had to stay. I continued going to clinic every day but I was starting to run out of certain medications. I had a lot of sick people with malaria, upper and lower respiratory tract infections, asthma, pregnant women etc… they all needed medications. I tried to do my best with what I had.

One week later week, I got invited to dinner by Italian catholic priests living on the other side of town. I drove to their house and was so surprised to get into an oasis of peace, beauty and abundance. They were growing their own coffee trees and other fruit trees. Their garden was beautiful. Their house was beautiful. Dinner was so incredibly delicious! I felt I was in heaven! What a contrast with our MSF house and our very simple meals. They were planning to go to Colombo the following day and offered me to travel with them. First, instead of driving East towards Vavuniya, they were planning on driving West towards the ocean. A boat was supposed to pick them up and take them to the closest harbor. They were planning on staying there for a while and slowly get on their way to Colombo. I really appreciated their offer and said I needed to contact Henry in Colombo to ask for authorization. I went to my car and tried calling Colombo. Fortunately, Henry was in the office and answered right away.

Me: "Hi, Henry, I am happy you're in your office!"

Henry: "All the MSF teams are back in Colombo, every single MSF personnel is back except for you. There is somebody close to the radio

24/7 just for you now. We are doing everything we can to get you out of Madhu but it is still too dangerous."

I told him about the priests' plan. He asked for more details and said he would get back to me in one hour. I went back to the priests' house. One hour later, I was back in my car for another radio contact.

Henry: "Chris, that's it, we have organized everything for you. Go with the priests tomorrow. Once you arrive at the harbor, the Sri Lankan army has agreed to pick you up and fly you back to Anurhadapura. An MSF vehicle will be waiting for you there."

I was thrilled but a little scared at the same time. It would be a long trip back to Colombo. I went back to the priests' house and with a big smile on my face, told them I had the OK from MSF Colombo to travel with them. They were very happy to be able to help. I thanked them for their delicious dinner and said goodbye. I had a hard time leaving their house. I felt so good and safe there.

That night I said goodbye to everybody. I had tears in my eyes. It was so hard to abandon the Sri Lankan personnel I had been working with for the last 3 months. Hopefully, they had learned enough and would be able to take over. I had just a few medications left and gave them the key of the pharmacy. I started packing. Late that night, I did a radio contact with Lars and told him my plan. Hopefully, I would be in his arms in a few days. Then, I went to bed and under my mosquito net, I dreamt about heaven. I had a lot of priests and angels flying around me and I was happy. This was my last night in Madhu.

The following day, at 6:00 am, I was ready to go. I did my last radio contact with Colombo. Everything was set and organized for my departure. A few seconds later, a large vehicle stopped in front of the house. The priests were there, picking me up. Their driver stepped out of the car to pick up my luggage and place it in the truck. All our local personnel had come to say a last goodbye. I had tears in my eyes. Who knows what was going to happen to them? I hoped they would be OK without our help. I hopped in at the back of the car and waived them goodbye as our vehicle left. It was the beginning of a very long and emotional trip.

It was a road I didn't know. I had taken roads East of Madhu but this time, we were heading West. I had heard that most roads around Madhu were mined. We were going slowly. The road was in very bad shape. Amazingly enough, I wasn't scared. I thought that nothing could happen to the vehicle of catholic priests. I felt much protected by God. God proved me right and after 3 hours of a very bumpy road, the ocean was in sight. As we got closer, I got more and more excited. I could see boats there. One of them was waiting for us. It was a very small one, barely big enough to fit all of us with our luggage. I was very grateful it could fit me. A few minutes later, 2 large Sri Lankan men started rowing and we left the shore. Two hours later we arrived at the harbor. A vehicle from the church was there to pick the priests up. I said goodbye to them and thanked them profusely. A vehicle from the army was there for me. I hopped in their vehicle.

They took me to a small air field where a helicopter was ready to take off. It was a military helicopter with no doors on either side. Instead of doors, there were gunmen, one gunman at each door. It was probably one of those helicopters that fired on Patricia, maybe even the same one. That thought horrified me. I had never been on a helicopter. The Sri Lankan sergeant told me to get in which I did with the help of the gunmen at the door.

To my amazement, there was no seat in the helicopter. Only the pilot and copilot had seats but at the back there was a big open space. The gunmen gave me a small wooden box for me to seat on and we took off. What a strange feeling to take off in a helicopter without doors. It felt like I could fall out at any time. After 15 minutes of flight, we started going down again. I heard shootings from the land below us. I couldn't believe it! We were going down in a battle field! How could the army do this to me! They were supposed to rescue me not to take me to a battle field! I got really scared. I thought it was the end of my life. I closed my eyes and mentally said goodbye to my parents, to Lars and to all the people I loved.

Gunshots from 2 feet away from me made me open my eyes again. The 2 gunmen near me at each door were shooting down. We were about 1,000 feet above ground and going down. Tigers in the forest around were shooting at us. Patricia was shot by a helicopter shooting at Tamil tigers and here I was in maybe the same copter shooting at tigers. I couldn't stop tears bursting out of my eyes. I felt completely helpless. Surrounded by gunshots, we landed in an open space in the forest. The gunmen near me were still shooting. As soon as we hit ground, about 20 army soldiers heavily armed hopped in around me. 1 minute later, we were taking off again. The gunmen at the doors were shooting continuously. As we got high enough, they stopped. I sighed with relief, happy to be still alive. I looked around me. The helicopter was now full of Sinhalese soldiers looking at me with curious eyes. Most were sitting on the floor, some were sitting on wooden boxes like me. I was right in the middle as far from each open door as I could.

One hour later, to my intense relief, we landed in Anurhadapura were a MSF vehicle was waiting for me. A few hours later we stopped in front of 24/4 Guildford Crescent. Oh what a relief! Henry was there greeting me. A lot of MSF people had gone back to France already. Patricia was in a hospital in Paris and was getting better. I needed to do a debriefing but before, I needed to freshen up. Henry gave me one hour. I put my suitcase in one of the bedrooms, went straight to the bathroom and run hot water in the bathtub..

My first hot bath in 3 months! What a delight! How heavenly! After 3 months of no electricity, no hot water, no bathtub, it felt out of this world to jump into a hot bath. It was like being on another planet or being dead and arriving in heaven. It was such an intense pleasure! Slowly I got in the tub, slowly I rubbed on my skin some nice smelling soap, and put some nice smelling shampoo in my hair. Slowly I lied down in the tub and stayed there for half an hour, breathing deeply, appreciating heaven as much as I could. Since that time, never again have I taken a hot bath for granted. Since that time, I have appreciated every single hot bath I have taken.

One hour later, I was in Henry's office for debriefing. I told him about the situation in Madhu and about my risky trip back to Colombo. He told me that the situation in Sri Lanka was bad with intensified fighting. Patricia's accident had been on the front page of all newspapers all over the world. France had decided to suspend diplomatic relationships with Sri Lanka. MSF was pulling out of the island. Henry had called my parents to reassure them but I needed to call them myself which I did a little later. One hour later, the phone rang. It was Lars. I was so happy to talk to him. We planned on having dinner together later that night.

It was 7 o'clock that night when Lars's white car arrived. I was out of the door and in his car in a few seconds. It was so wonderful to see him again. It was like being in a dream. He was exactly as I remembered him, tall, slim, with beautiful blue eyes. He took me to the same Chinese restaurant we went to 3 months prior. We had a long talk. I told him about my 3 months in Madhu and the frightening trip back to Colombo. He told me about his work and about the situation from his point of view.

At the end, he asked me: "What are your plans for the future?"

Me: "I don't know yet, Lars, everybody is being flown back to France so, I guess I should fly back then rest at my parents' house and then go on another MSF mission."

That's when he said: "If you want, you can stay at my house. My assignment is for another year and my wife is staying in Norway. You can have the guest bedroom as long as you want."

It only took me one second to think then I said: "I would like that Lars. It would be great to stay with you."

Lars: "Do you want to move in tonight?"

The question surprised me. Wasn't this a little soon? How would the MSF people take this? But then, I thought about the MSF house which was always noisy and full of people. Lars's house was big and quiet and

I really wanted to put all the MSF adventure behind me. I needed rest and peace. Deep in my heart, I really wanted to move in with Lars as soon as possible. I explained all my thoughts to Lars and concluded: "tonight would be great!"

As we came back from the restaurant, Lars dropped me off at 24/4 Guildford Crescent but instead of leaving, he waited in his car. I dashed out of the car and under the astonished eyes of Henry and the MSF team, I started packing, saying I was going to stay with Lars for a while. I didn't know yet when I was going to fly back to France.

I stayed one month with Lars. It was wonderful. I was on vacation and was doing absolutely nothing during the day. The truth is that I needed rest. A very nice Sri Lanken couple was working for Lars, cooking for him, cleaning the house and washing his clothes. I had absolutely nothing to do. I was like a princess. It was a great feeling! Every morning I had a fresh coconut for breakfast which was just delicious. It was also very nourishing and contained a lot of calories which is something I only realized when I couldn't fit in my jeans any more. I had to cut back on coconuts then my jeans started fitting again. I still to this day enjoy a fresh coconut for breakfast from time to time.

Lars would go to work everyday. During that time, I would have a long breakfast, then a long hot bath. You can guess how much I really appreciated those hot baths! The whole house was air conditioned and I appreciated that as well after 3 months in Madhu without air conditioning. During the day, I would go for a walk and relax. At night, when Lars would come back from work we would play table tennis or tennis then we would have dinner either at the house (thanks to his cooks) or in a nice restaurant. It was heavenly for me. It was much less heavenly for Lars whom I noticed was getting more and more tired. He was 15 years older than me and it was starting to show. After his work day, he had less and less energy left for me. That's when he decided to take a week of vacation. One morning he asked me: "How would you like to go to the Maldives Islands with me?" I jumped up with excitement and said I would love it. At the end of the week, we were flying to the Maldives. We stayed in Kurumba Island one week and had the most wonderful time. Lars taught me how to snorkel and we played tennis a lot. We had delicious buffet breakfasts, lunches and dinners. Lars could finally relax and enjoy our being together. We were very happy. The week went by very fast and soon is was time for us to fly back to Colombo.

When we came back to Colombo, I started accompanying Lars on his business trips as a Norwegian diplomat. I accompanied him to Batticaloa and Trincomalee. We visited Sri Lankan officials and refugee camps there. Life as the "fiancée" of a diplomat was very different from life as a physician working in a refugee camp. I actually loved both. On our way, we also visited Pollonarua where Lars took a picture of me in front of a large lying Buddha and Kandy were we visited tea plantations. We had a great time. Little did I know that we were close to the end of our time together.

We had come back from Trincomalee the previous week and Lars had just left for work. After a great breakfast, long bath and nice walk, I was in the middle of the living room when suddenly I heard a huge loud blast. I closed my eyes and heard glass breaking then more glass breaking then water falling. When I opened my eyes again, I saw broken glass all around me. As I was looking around I saw that all the windows had broken. Fortunately I was in the middle of the living room so no broken glass had hurt me. Unfortunately water pipes had exploded and water was falling from the ceiling. Paralyzed, I waited to see if any other explosion would happen but there was only silence. 5 minutes later, the phone rang. It was Lars.

Lars: "Chris, are you O.K.? You are not injured?

I reassured him and told him I was O.K but that all the windows had broken and that a water pipe had exploded.

He then explained: "A Tamil vehicle full with explosives just exploded outside the Sinhalese army headquarters which is very close to the house. The whole area is destroyed. I am leaving right now to be with you and assess the damage."

Three hours later, Lars was still not home. All the roads were blocked. There was panic everywhere. The whole area, half a mile around the army headquarters, was in ruins. There were a lot of injured and dead people. Ambulances were starting to arrive. A two-miles circle was rapidly controlled by the army.

As I was waiting for Lars, a thought suddenly came to me: We say never twice without a third time. The first time was when our vehicle in Madhu got under attack by the Sinhalese army. I was the one supposed to be in it but fortunately, I wasn't. The second time was this explosion. Both times, I was safe but there might be a third time later and that time, I might not be safe any more. It was time for me to go back to Paris and stop working for MSF for a while. As for Lars, he was married and he never told me he wanted to leave his wife for me. We were very happy together but I knew it was just temporary. Anyways, I wasn't ready to get into a forever relationship. It was time to leave Sri Lanka. The only thing is that I would have liked to go to India. Madras was so close to Sri Lanka. Maybe I could go to Madras next week and then fly back to Paris.

It was late when finally Lars made it home. He explained that all the roads were blocked and there were traffic jams everywhere. He assessed the damage of the house. Together, we started getting the broken glass out. That same day, as we were having dinner home, I told him it was time for me to leave. He understood.

The following couple of days, I helped him around the house then bought a plane ticket for Madras, India. I stayed there one week, resting and shopping. It was a great feeling to be in India. I loved Madras. I fell in love with silk saris and Indian shoes. I bought 3 saris and 3 pairs of shoes. One week later, I was back in Colombo, thinking I would stay another couple of weeks with Lars then fly back to Paris.

That's when I got THE call: It was a panic phone call from my mother in Paris: "Chris, your Dad has been in a hospital in Paris for 3 weeks and yesterday, a procedure went wrong, he is now in intensive care unit on a ventilator, I am so scared! Can you come?"

I said goodbye to Lars and took the first flight out of Colombo.

Working for Doctors Without Borders in Sri Lanka

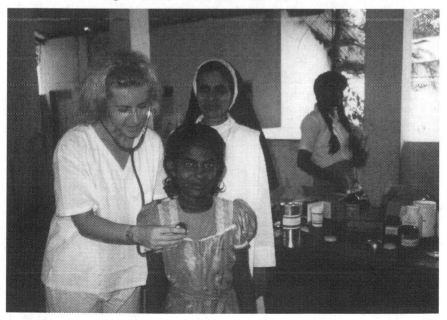

Examining patients in Madhu, Sri Lanka

# Chapter 8
# Trying to save Dad

Twelve hours later, I was at Dad's bedside in the Intensive Care Unit of one of the main hospitals in Paris. Dad looked very emaciated, his arms and hands were all bruised from all the needle sticks. His eyes were closed and his breathing was regulated by a ventilator. I asked to talk to the physician who was in charge of him. He was of no help at all! He didn't know what my father had. He wasn't sure of the diagnosis and had no idea of the way to treat him or of the prognosis. I had to step in! I had all the time in the world. I had just taken care of 20,000 people in a refugee camp, I had a lot of energy and felt very powerful.

I asked to see his medical chart and started studying it. It was a big chart. I just couldn't believe it. Dad had never been sick before. What was happening? What was his diagnosis? What was the prognosis? It took me 4 hours to read the whole chart and study the different blood test results. It seemed that 3 months prior, Dad had blood in his stools. He didn't think much of it and thought it was just blood from hemorrhoids. One month later, he started having more bloody stools and made an appointment to see a gastroenterologist. That's when he started running a low grade fever and had to cancel his appointment. He was feeling very tired with a low grade fever everyday. Since he had a heart murmur (which had been known for several years), he was afraid of having endocarditis (infection of one of the heart valves). He then made an appointment with one of the best cardiologists in Paris. That cardiologist diagnosed a possible endocarditis and decided to hospitalize him right away for 3 weeks of IV antibiotics. Blood tests diagnosed septicemia from a bug that I had never heard about. Three weeks of antibiotics completely destroyed all his veins. Both his arms and legs were black and blue with bruises and it was getting difficult to find a new vein each day. Since Dad was still complaining of bloody stools, the medical team decided to do a colonoscopy. Unfortunately they did it without anesthesia or sedation. The gastroenterologist kept on forcing the colonoscopy tube forward despite the pain that my father was having. As my father was screaming because of the pain, the specialist kept pushing. That's when my father lost consciousness, had to be intubated and ventilated.

As I was reading the chart, I felt anger building up. At the end, I was so angry, I had to leave the hospital and go for a walk. Three months of blood in his stools and nobody had diagnosed anything!!! For me, it was obvious that there was a digestive cancer somewhere. It is well known that colon cancer can give septicemias if it is not diagnosed early. This was probably the explanation of the rare bug in his blood. I looked at the result of the echocardiogram. There was no vegetation seen on any valve. All this time lost while a nasty digestive cancer was probably growing!!! The problem is that if you go and see a cardiologist, he will concentrate his attention on cardiology issues and will probably miss any other problem. That is what happened. Had my father gone to see a gastroenterologist instead of a cardiologist, the diagnosis would have been different. As I was walking back to the ICU, I started cooling down. The past was past. Now, I needed to focus on the present and the future. I was sure there was a cancer somewhere. We had to find it.

I came back to room # 4 of the ICU. Dad was getting agitated. I started talking to him: "Dad, it's me, Chris, I came back from Sri Lanka. I am here for you now. You'll get better! I'll get you out of this!" As I was talking, he opened his eyes and looked at me. He looked very worried and agitated. He started moving his head as if he wanted to get rid of the tube that was making him breathe. I said: "Dad, do you want us to get the breathing tube out?" He nodded his head meaning yes. I told him to relax and that I was going to talk to one of the physicians to get his breathing tube out.

I walked out of room # 4 and found the physician on call that evening. I explained the situation but he refused to extubate him. He said it might be too hard for Dad's heart. He wanted to wait until the following day.

I went back to Dad's bedside and explained to him what the physician had said. He looked very disappointed. I asked him more questions. Was he in pain? Did he need to go to the bathroom? He shook his head indicated no. I told him to relax, tomorrow would come fast and soon, he would be able to talk and walk. It was hard to leave him that night.

I went back to Bourg-La-Reine to stay with Mom. I told her all about my day with Dad. She didn't go to the hospital to see him. She was suffering from a strange condition I called Hospital Allergy. In my life, I have seen very few people with this rare condition. She couldn't get into a hospital without feeling nauseated and dizzy. She had to get out immediately. While I was in Sri Lanka, she did visit Dad but it was physically very hard for her because of her condition. Now that I was in France, she didn't want to go to the hospital any more. She told me: "Chris, in the future, if I am sick, never put me in a hospital. You'll need to treat me at home. In a hospital, I'll die."

It was great to be home again but in the house, there was a strange feeling of emptiness. We were missing Dad.

The following day, I went to the hospital again, hoping the medical team had extubated him. As I entered the ICU, I got a huge shock. Nurses and doctors were running toward room # 4. A defibrillator was being run there. One doctor was doing chest compressions. Tears came to my eyes: Did Dad just pass away? How can this be? What happened? I should have come earlier! Maybe I could have prevented that! As I came closer to the room, I saw a heavy set body lying on the bed. The patient didn't look like my Dad at all. I asked one of the nurses. She said: "Dr. Gilbert, your Dad has been moved to room # 7. He is doing well." I sighed with relief. Till this day I remember those minutes in the ICU.

As I went towards room # 7, I saw Dad lying there. His eyes were open but he was still intubated. He seemed very happy to see me. He answered my questions with shaking his head. He was not in pain; he had enough of the breathing machine and wanted to be extubated. I went to the physician in charge and asked for Dad to be extubated. The physician refused again saying that it might be too hard for his heart. He wanted to wait until the following day again. I had read the entire chart the previous day and I thought his heart was good enough to extubate. I tried to convince him. I said I was going to stay at his bedside for a few hours. This was a good time to do it. I insisted so much that the physician finally agreed to do it. A few minutes later, Dad was extubated.

What a relief! Finally he could breathe by himself! Finally he could talk! He thanked me. He had no problem breathing and the rest of the evening, I took care of him, humidifying his lips and talking to him, making sure he was O.K. You see, when you are a medical doctor, you are not supposed to take care of your family but Dad and I had to. We had no choice. When we are faced with medical mistakes from other physicians, we have to intervene for each other. When I was a child and later when I was in a hospital for my back, Dad took excellent care of me. I, too, would take excellent care of him.

One day later, he was able to eat, drink and walk again. He had lost a lot of weight and was very weak.

Now, I had to strategize. I was convinced there was a cancer somewhere in his body. I had to find it. I talked to his doctors. They offered to do a colonoscopy again. I refused. Dad had fainted during the first one. I was not in favor of doing a second one. We opted for something less aggressive, a radiological exam called barium enema. I asked and obtained permission to be with Dad for all the future procedures. After what had happened during the colonoscopy, I was not about to leave him by himself for any procedure anymore. I wanted to double check everything to make sure he was safe.

We went down to the radiology department getting ready for the barium enema. The technician started pushing barium up. Dad started being in pain right away. As the technician continued without slowing down, I saw Dad about to faint again. I had to tell the technician to stop. We had to wait a few minutes until Dad was ready for the procedure to continue. Several times, I had to tell the technician to stop. Scary, isn't it? Had I not been there, Dad would have fainted again and would have been intubated again and we would have been back to square one with another intubation and no diagnosis. Each patient needs very special care and attention. Hospitals with so many patients, so many doctors, nurses and technicians are not the best places for such a special attention. As we managed to get to the end of the enema slowly but surely, I went to the screen. I was stunned to see that there was a large mass obstructing the right colon. I was right, this was probably a cancer. We had found it. Dad needed surgery as soon as possible!

I contacted the surgeon, showed him the X-Rays and explained the case. He agreed to operate one week later. It would give him one week to recuperate. I explained everything to Dad who agreed. I asked the surgeon if I could be in the operating room at the time of surgery. He said yes. I wanted to be in the room to see the extent of the damage, to assess any possible metastasis and to make immediate decisions if such needed to be made.

The following week, Dad got stronger and it looked like he would be able to have surgery.

The following Monday, we were both in the operating room. The surgeon was ready. When he said: "Scalpel", my heart started beating rapidly. I was wondering how advanced his cancer was. We would know in a few minutes.

Soon after, I was relieved. The surgeon found a cancer which was limited to the right colon. It was a large tumor almost completely obstructing the lumen (which explained why the colonoscopy and the barium enema had been so painful) but there was no metastasis to any lymph node or anywhere else in his body. The surgeon did a right hemicolectomy which means that he resected the right half of the colon.

I was at Dad's bedside when he woke up after surgery and immediately reassured him: "Dad, we found your cancer and everything bad was removed. You are cured. You should get better quickly." Dad smiled saying thank you. I called Mom immediately to reassure her too.

Dad had a hard time staying in the hospital. It was too noisy and got on his nerves. I managed to convince the surgeon that I could take care of him myself at home. Dad was so happy to be back home after almost 2 months in the hospital. After taking care of 20,000 people in a refugee camp, I was happy to take care of just one very special patient, Dad.

Dad was improving everyday and his surgical wound was healing nicely. He had the best possible home care. The house was quiet, Mom was cooking for him and I was doing his dressings every day.

After one month, he was completely back to normal. We went to see his surgeon to decide what to do next. He told us that Dad didn't have to go through chemotherapy or radiation therapy. He just needed a follow-up in 6 months. That turned out to be a mistake but we didn't know it at the time. Had we known what we know now, we would have done a few rounds of chemotherapy. Unfortunately, we didn't do anything and just waited. This was great for Dad who started enjoying life again. Mom and he started traveling again. It was time for me to go back to work. I wasn't ready to work for MSF just yet. I needed easy work and decided to call Club Med.

It was July 14th in France and fireworks were everywhere, celebrating Bastille Day. As I heard the first fireworks, I jumped and got scared. Were we under attack? Was I in danger? I had to mentally reassure myself. There was no danger, it was only fireworks! I still had to block my ears to prevent myself from hearing. I had no idea that after my mission in Sri Lanka, I wouldn't be able to hear fireworks any more. I started to understand what post traumatic stress disorder meant. Those fireworks sounded so much like the shootings and bombings I had heard everyday in Madhu for 3 months. It took me several years to be able to appreciate fireworks again.

# Chapter 9
# Working in Asia

## *Summer 1991*

In Paris, I was listening to the news on the radio several times a day. That summer, I started being interested in what was happening in China. Torrential rains were flooding the Anhui province. I was thinking that it would be great if MSF was getting involved. It was time for me to work for MSF again but I didn't want a war zone any more. I had seen enough of war. China would be great.

I called MSF to tell them I would be interested in a China mission if there were to be one. They said they would keep me in mind.

One day, as I was listening to the news again, I heard that the situation in China was getting worse. 400,000 people were displaced, their homes being destroyed by raising waters. China was asking for international help. MSF was getting involved, planning to send medical supplies and tents. They were also going to send one physician and one nurse to assess the situation. That was my cue. I didn't listen any more. It was time to go to MSF headquarters. One physician wasn't much. What were my chances? I probably didn't have much chance since I didn't speak Chinese nor did I have experience in floods. But it didn't hurt to ask.

As I entered MSF headquarters, the person responsible for physician assignments came to me: "Chris, didn't you request to go to China if we were sending a medical team?" I said yes. She then said: "Well it is your mission if you want it. We need a physician to leave in a couple of days. Can you be available that fast?" I said yes. I was ecstatic. The mission was mine!!!

The rest of the afternoon and the following day, I was briefed on what to do. The following day, I started learning Chinese. Two days later I was on the plane to Beijing.

In Beijing, I met the rest of the team: a nurse Brigitte, a logistician and a coordinator who spoke fluent Mandarin. We took a small plane to get to Anhui province. There, we stayed in hotels in Hefei and Yingshang and from there, everyday, Chinese officials took us to different flooded towns to assess the damage.

Over 150,000 people were still displaced. It was a spectacular site. The Hwai He River was too high. All houses were under water and we had to travel by boat. I bought high purple plastic boots. The sanitary situation was bad. We were afraid of cholera outbreaks. Chinese officials were doing a great job. Over 100 Chinese medical teams had been created. I was planning to visit most of them, check and improve their training and bring them the medications they needed most. I got busy very quickly, visiting sites everyday and writing reports at night. I visited the main 4 districts: Feng Tai, Shou Xian, Ying Shang and Huo Qiu along the rivers Huai He and Pi. In Feng Tai and Huo Qiu, there were a lot of cases of diarrhea, upper respiratory tract infections, conjunctivitis and cutaneous infections. In Shou Xian and Huo Qiu there was a lot of hepatitis. We brought thousands of tents, food supplies (half a kilogram of rice and wheat per person per day) and chlorinated tablets to disinfect drinking water. We helped organize water tanks, latrines and holes in the ground for trash. We helped eradicate rats, flies and mosquitoes in order to prevent diseases like cholera and malaria. We brought antibiotics, anti-diarrhea tablets and drinking rehydration fluids. We distributed clothes and blankets to get the people ready for a very cold winter. We needed to act fast.

The Anhui province was not open to tourism. The local Chinese people had never seen a blond woman in real life. I was blond, thin, and pretty. Needless to say that everybody was looking at me. In the evenings, as I was back in my hotel, I would go out for grocery and clothes shopping. I had learned enough Chinese to get by without a translator. As I was walking in the streets by myself, everybody would stare at me. Men would stop their bicycles in the middle of the street to look at me. This would amuse me to no end. One evening, a man was going fast on his bicycle when he suddenly saw me. It seems that he just saw an extra terrestrial. He couldn't take his eyes off me and while his head was turning focusing on me, his bicycle didn't follow. With a big bang, he fell off his bicycle. As I was getting ready to run towards him, he got up in a few seconds, got back on his bicycle and pedaled away quickly. This made me laugh. As for the restroom episodes, I will remember them my whole life.

Restrooms in the middle of the countryside in the Anhui province were very unique. There was of course a side for women and a side for men. In the side for women, all you had were holes in the ground. Most often there were 4 or 5 holes in the ground in line and a few feet apart from each other. In each hole were moving thousands of huge worms or maggots crawling on top of each other. The first time I looked inside the hole, I almost vomited but I had diarrhea that day so fortunately, I didn't have time to think too much. I had to go. The following times, I tried not to look inside the holes. The separations between the holes were accomplished by a one foot high "wall". Not much privacy, you would say. Well you are right. There was no privacy at all. And guess what, each time I wanted to go to the restroom, at least 3 other women wanted to go too. All the other holes were occupied each time and each of the other women stooping was looking at me, looking at my blond hair and trying to see if I was blond everywhere. They were looking at me as if I was an extraterrestrial. At the beginning I was shocked but then, I got used to it. At the end, I thought it was funny.

I stayed 3 months in China. Then the situation got much better and waters started to recede. It was time to leave.

After the end of my mission, I decided to stay a few days in China to visit Shanghai, Beijing and the Great Wall. I had a wonderful time, bought the equivalent of half a suitcase of silk clothes (underwear, blouses, pants and scarves). They were so cheap and so beautiful! I walked long hours inside the Forbidden City in Beijing. I walked endlessly along the Great Wall of China which beauty amazed me. I couldn't stop taking pictures. All the views were breathtaking. I did all this by myself. I was used to traveling alone. For me traveling with friends was not appealing. I was much better alone.

After being a tourist in China for 2 weeks, I was still not ready to go home. I was interested in going to Vietnam. I heard MSF had a mission in Vietnam. I tried to contact them to see if I could come and visit. After all, I was so close to them! The chief of the Vietnamese mission answered right away: "You were on an MSF mission in China and you just finished your mission? Sure you can come and visit us. You are welcome to stay with us. We'll take you with us on our hospital rounds."

I said: "Thank you so much! I would love that! I'll reserve my plane ticket right away!"

Half an hour later, I was at a local Beijing travel agency, getting a plane ticket for Hanoi, Vietnam via Bangkok.

On flights, I usually get up very often to stretch my legs and spend a lot of time standing at the back of the plane. There I usually meet people who do the same. Well, on the flight from Bangkok to Hanoi, I met 3 very interesting men.

First, I met David Ignatius, American journalist writing for the Washington Post and author of several books. He gave me one of his books and signed it for me. It was fascinating talking to him. I had seen him the previous month in Beijing but I didn't talk to him then. We were both traveling a lot for our jobs. I realized that the world was in fact very small. The world itself had become my country.

On the same flight, I met a Japanese business man who was flying to Vietnam to buy cheap goods that he was going to resell in Japan for a much higher price. I talked to him for a while too. It was interesting to have his perspective of the world.

The 3rd man I met was an American man who was coming back to Vietnam after 20 years. The last time he was in Northern Vietnam was during the Vietnam War, 20 years earlier. That was where he had lost some of his best friends. He had to come back. There was so much emotion attached to his coming back that day! It was fascinating to talk to him. Yes, this plane was a crossroad of lives, all different and powerful lives, experiences and emotions. The common point of all of us was that we were all world travelers. The world had become our country.

The arrival in Hanoi was very special. Security was tight and there was very little luxury at the airport. It was obvious this wasn't a popular tourist destination. I stayed a couple of days in Hanoi then flew to Hue, 600 km south of Hanoi. At Hue airport, Claude, the mission coordinator from MSF Vietnam was waiting for me and took me to the MSF house. We immediately connected. He had spent a lot of time in Mozambique too and we had a lot to talk about. He introduced me to Nadia, the MSF physician. We immediately became friends and I started helping her at the Hue hospital. I discovered the problems of working in a communist country where everybody earns the same low salary. There was no incentive for people to work more, longer hours and do a better job. MSF was trying to improve the medical care, get the emergency room to be open longer hours, give local nurses and doctors better more effective drugs and ways to diagnose and treat. But changes were not easily welcome. Why would they have to work more for the same pay? In the hospital, people would do their job slowly without hurrying and without working extra hours. Forget about taking care of a dying man if it wasn't during normal work hours. Forget about trying to improve medical care. The pay would be the same anyway. There was no incentive. It created a stunning passivity everywhere.

My second week, we visited local small MSF dispensaries along the Laguna. It was amazing to hear a lot of people being able to speak and understand French, especially the older people. Vietnam had been a French colony in the past and this had left a strong imprint.

The weather was gorgeous with blue sky and temperature around 75 degrees F. Since he had some vacation time, Claude decided to take me to the beautiful Hue Forbidden City and its tumes. The following day, we went to Da Nang and gorgeous old town of Hoi An. I fell in love with Vietnam. It was one of the most beautiful countries I had ever seen with its spectacular mountains near the seaside, its beautiful beaches near rice fields, banana plantations, papaya trees and lekima trees. It is hard for me to describe the scenery other than pure beauty. I took a lot of pictures that I admire to this day. By the way, lekimas were new fruits to me. They looked like persimmons but tasted like sweet potatoes. They were delicious. My last day, we had dinner in a pagoda. It was a sumptuous vegetarian dinner prepared by monks. The artistic presentation of each dish was unique and its taste was so incredibly good. I fell in love with Vietnamese food that I love to this day. I fell in love with the people of Vietnam. They were so sweet and had suffered so much. They were all very scared, especially afraid to talk to us, afraid there would be consequences and that they would be put in jail for talking too much. They were so afraid of the regime. I discovered hard core communism and promised myself I would never live in a communist country. The theory of communism was not a bad one in itself but the live example that I saw was pure horror in such a paradise country.

I was learning so much! Before working for MSF, I didn't know very much about life or about the world. I was catching on quickly.

The day I flew back to Paris, I wished I had spent more time in Vietnam. I really and truly loved that country.

Working for Doctors Without Borders in China

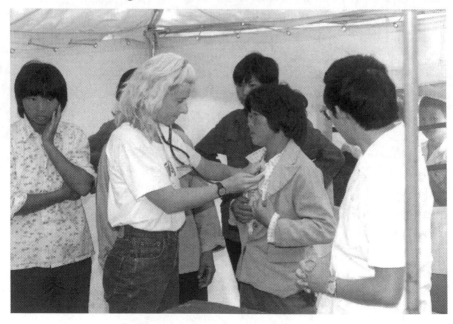

Examining patients in China

# Chapter 10
# Working in the Caribbean then competing for "Miss Winter Olympic Games 1992"

Coming back from Vietnam, I rested one week in Paris, then in spring 1992, I contacted Club Med again to see if any exciting destination was available. I needed a break from MSF.

As I was talking to the Club Med recruiter, she said: "Chris, I need a physician to accept a 4 months contract touring several Club Meds for safety inspections, would you be available?"

"Of course" I replied, "this would be great, but I have never done any safety inspection before, what does the job consist of?" She explained I would have to spend one to 2 weeks in each Club Med in the Caribbean Islands. The first part of my job would be to examine all the GOs to make sure they were healthy and fit for their work. The second part of my work would be to inspect all the kitchens, bars, nightclubs and sport activity areas to make sure everything was safe and had a good level of sanitation. I had to take samples of tap water, ice cube water, swimming pool water and send those to the lab. I would have to write a complete report about each facility. This was new for me but I loved challenges. I was also very excited by the destinations. I would have to fly to each Club Med in the Caribbean Island! There were in Florida, the Bahamas, Turcs and Caicos, the Dominican Republic, St Martin,

Martinique, Guadeloupe and St Lucia. How exotic! Of course, the pay wasn't much as usual but all the flights were paid for, I could eat at all the buffets just like tourists do and I could participate in any sport activity I wanted as if I was a paying tourist from the resort. The offer was too good to refuse. I accepted.

The following week, I was flying to the Dominican Republic for my first Club Med inspection. In the mornings, I examined the GOs who were all between 18 and 27 years old and extremely physically fit. It was actually a lot of fun to examine those strong gorgeous muscular men and women. In the afternoons I inspected all the buildings, made sure there was no fire hazard, inspected refrigerators, freezers, bars, kitchen counters, toilets, took samples of water and checked that all sport activities were safely supervised. I made sure kitchen personnel were wearing plastic gloves when touching food. I visited kitchens unexpectedly at 2.00 am to make sure that all food was wrapped away and that there were no rats running around. I checked that all lights outside at night were bright enough for people not to trip on stairs and that stairs were well marked. In the evenings, I wrote reports. I learned a lot during those 4 months about public health and security requirements. I enjoyed those 4 months tremendously. I had 3 to 4 hours off per day which allowed me to participate in local sports activities and I enjoyed delicious buffets 3 times a day. I was very welcome by all the Club Med GOs everywhere and it was a pleasure to get to know everybody.

I did the same routine in each island, making sure I had enough time to visit each island on my off hours. The Turks and Caicos islands were 575 miles Southwest of Miami and had the 3rd largest coral reef system in the world. I was impressed by the their pristine white sandy beaches and crystal clear turquoise waters. The difference with the other islands is that they were mostly flat without mountains or volcanos. I learned how to scuba dive for the first time and I met Jean-Michel Cousteau and his team who were shooting a movie. Turkoise, the Turks Club Med was famous at the time for its wild dolphin called Jojo. This dolphin was known to want to have fun. He would swim under the skis of the people who were learning how to waterski and would make them fall. He was also known to love women who were on their period. He would swim next to them and get all excited. Well, during my stay in Turkoise, I jumped in the water as often as possible to try to see him but I only saw him once from far away. That is one thing I missed in Turkoise. I would have loved to spend more time there and to play with Jojo. Oh well, you cannot have everything.

In St Martin, I bought my first video camera and started filming and in Guadeloupe, I went to visit the beautiful small islands called "Les Saintes". They were just pure paradise. In Martinique, I went back to Lamentin Hospital were I had worked one year during my medical internship. I was surprised to see that a lot of constructions had changed the hospital which was now more modern. I could only find one physician that I knew and was surprised to see how much weight he had gained.

The weather was wonderful, hot and humid, the way I loved it. Each island and each Club Med had its own charm. The only thing that was a little unsettling is that in each Club, after two weeks, I had a lot of friends to whom I had to say goodbye to fly to the next Club. After one to 2 weeks in this other Club, I would get attached to other people to whom I had to say goodbye too and so on. But I didn't mind. This 4 months experience was unforgettable.

My last Club was in Sandpiper, Florida. There I arrived just before a hurricane warning. I had never seen such a thing. All boats had to be secured and all windows had to be protected by wooden boards. The preparation for hurricane was spectacular. At the last minute, that hurricane changed directions and Sandpiper was spared. It was also time for me to fly back to Paris. My work was over.

As I was arriving in Paris, the Club Med recruiter called me. She urgently needed somebody to work for one month in Les Menuires in the French Alps. It was a busy ski resort. This was in 1992, the year France was hosting the Winter Olympic Games. And guess what, Les Menuires Club Med was supposed to host the athletes for one day. Was I available to go there? Well, of course I was! Who would refuse such a destination at such a time? I was starting to love those hard core contrasts, alternating between MSF work in poor needy famined countries and Club Med work in rich overfed countries.

Within one week, I was in the French Alps. Until now, all my missions had been in hot weather destinations. Snow was a big change for me. The Olympic games made it well worth while. I treated broken legs, sprained ankles and knees. I started skiing again on my off duty hours. Being in Les Menuires during the French Alps winter Olympics was a real treat. I'll never forget that. The day the athletes used our Resort for rest, was awesome. I felt like I was becoming part of History. Things became even more memorable when the media started advertising about Miss Olympic Games 1992. Yes, there would be a contest for who would be the most beautiful girl that winter. There was only one problem – Could the organizers get enough contestants? So, guess what they did? They went to us, Club Med GOs to ask us if we were willing to become contestants. One of my close friends working as a nurse looked at me and said: "Chris, I'll do it if you do it too". I was astonished. Me, a very average girl competing to be Miss Olympic Games 1992!!!? I told the organizers that I didn't think I was beautiful enough. They said they didn't care. They just needed more girls. So, my girlfriend and I accepted. Now that was something! I had accepted this work only to rest after my MSF mission in China and here I was competing for the title of Miss Olympic Games 1992. This was mind blowing to me.

That's when the fun started. I had to learn how to walk with super high heels. I had to get a super fancy outfit and super fancy make-up. I took it as a game. I never intended to win and in fact I didn't win but it certainly was a lot of fun to be on TV.

The rest of the month went by very fast. Pretty soon, it was time to go back to Paris. I said goodbye to all the GOs, put in my suitcase the super warm wool sweater and the beautiful fur boots I had just bought and left for the train station. By the way, this super warm wool sweater has been my favorite sweater to this day. It has the combination of my 2 favorite colors purple and turquoise, I still now wear it very often and bring it on most of my trips.

Competing in the French Alpes for the title
of Miss Olympic Games 1992

# Chapter 11
# Working in Mauritania

I spent one week in Paris, resting after all this travel then I contacted MSF again in November 1992. After working in luxurious areas where food was abundant, it was time for me to work in a refugee camp again and donate my time to the poor. MSF told me that they needed a physician to work in Mauritania at the boarder of Mali. It was a refugee camp filled with Touareg people, in the middle of the desert. Again, I accepted right away. I had never met any Touareg people. All I knew was that Touaregs were nomads traveling on camels.

One week later, I was in Nouakchott, Mauritania, picked up at the airport by a local MSF driver. 2 days later, we were heading East in a four-wheel drive vehicle. As soon as we got out of Nouakchott, we got into sand dunes territory, miles and miles of sand dunes. It was the Sael desert. It was beautiful and I fell in love with it. We drove 1,300 kilometers! 1,300 kilometers of dunes with different shades of golden and grey sand! From time to time, we saw people on camels but most of the time, we were the only ones on the road. It was one of the most beautiful scenes I had ever viewed. I remember it to this day. From time to time, I would ask the driver to stop because I needed to empty my bladder. Those Moments were magic. I would walk away from our vehicle and walk into the sand dunes for my private Moment. We had to spend 2 nights camping out. I spent them looking at the bright stars of the sky and listening to the silence of the desert.

1,300 kilometers later, we arrived in Bassikounou. It was a small town in the middle of nowhere. Men were dressed with white or blue wide pants and long wide shirts. They all had a large and long scarf rolled several times around their head and covering their mouth. We went by the refugee camp covered with tents and arrived at the MSF house. It was a small house with cement floors. The rooms were very small. I met the nurses, physician and logistician I was going to work with. I immediately knew it would be a difficult mission for me. I immediately knew I would be miserable.

Miserable I was! The whole team was smoking cigarettes heavily. Nurses, physician, logistician, everybody got together for meetings and meals and smoked. All the rooms of the house were full of smoke. I was the only nonsmoker! In a lot of my previous missions, several members of the team were smokers. It was unfortunately very common for MSF people, but it was the first time that I was the only nonsmoker living with heavy smokers. I was clearly a minority. Forget about asking everybody not to smoke for me. I tried but it didn't work. I had a lot of difficulty getting along with my team. As for my bedroom, it was so small that after putting a small mattress on the cement floor, I only had room for one suitcase and that was all. It was also very noisy, next to the dining room where everybody was staying up late at night to talk, smoke cigarettes and listen to music until 2 or 3 am. I, on the other hand, needed to be asleep at 10:00 pm in order to rest after busy work days. It was not a good situation.

The refugee camp was busy and a lot of adults and children refugees were having acute diarrhea with dehydration. We had to place IVs in a lot of them and educate people to prevent the infectious diarrhea to spread to the whole camp. We also had to vaccinate children, make sure they were fed adequately and organize a program for pregnant women. It was busy and I was exhausted.

After my first week of misery, I noticed that outside of the MSF house, on the other side of the street, was a small cement house which only had one room, a larger room which was empty. I asked the team if I could move there. They said that I could do it if I was not afraid. I would be more isolated, with no restroom around and nobody to protect me in case I was in danger. I didn't care. All I needed was a private room large enough for me to walk a few steps, isolated from the smoking and noisy team.

The following day, I packed everything and moved to my new room. There I was instantaneously happier. It was quiet and there was no smoke. I had room to walk around my bed. Although I was isolated, I wasn't too scared. I had to get up once or twice per night to go to the bathroom. I would get out of my room, go outside with my flashlight, walk a few feet, and make sure there was no scorpion or other dangerous insect or man around and I would pee in a sand dune. Soon my life became more livable and organized. I bought Touareg pants for myself and learned how to use those long scarves wrapped around the head and mouth. Believe me, you learn those things very quickly when you experience your first sandstorm. Winds can be very strong in the desert and sand starts flying everywhere. Quickly I learned how to wrap the scarf around my head, nose and mouth so that only my eyes were in the open air.

I also learned how to eat with my fingers. We had a welcome dinner where the locals killed a sheep for us and roasted it. Roasted sheep and rice was the utmost delicious meal there and it was truly unforgettably tasty. The locals were eating with their fingers and we did the same. Then we would have mint tea with them. It was a strong tea with a lot of sugar. We had to be careful to only eat cooked food and only drink boiled water. We had to refuse anything that was not cooked or boiled because there was too much risk of infection.

One day, the veterinarians who were living at the other end of the refugee camp, came to me asking if I wanted a baby sheep. They had just delivered it but its mother had died shortly after giving birth. They couldn't keep it and it was about to get roasted for dinner. Every body knew that I loved animals since on my days off, I would go to the local market and watch camels and sheep with their babies. I decided to adopt the baby sheep. He was 60 % black and 40 % white and adopted me as his Mommy immediately. He was so cute. I called him Atar which means star in the local language. Atar would follow me everywhere and stay near my feet all the time, except when there were smokers around. And boy were there smokers around! His favorite thing was to eat cigarettes butts! He had a particular taste for those and even though I tried to teach him not to eat them, he would eat them anyways. Atar was getting along well with the team's dog. It was fun to see them play together.

There were 15,700 people in the refugee camp and we had to organize food, water, latrines, tents, vaccinations, care for pregnant women, care for children, clinics for preventative care and clinics for curative care. We had one building for general clinics, one tent for ob-gyn clinics, another tent for deliveries and two tents for hospitalization. With 80 to 100 persons lining up in front of our clinic every day, we were extremely busy and time went by fast. Refugees were living under tents donated by the Red Cross and the European Community.

I loved those Touareg nomads. They were very strong, used to live on milk and meat only, used to walk miles and miles everyday and used to live through sandstorms. I became very attached to them and admired them a lot. They used to live in Mali but had been thrown out of that country by the Malian army and had asked for Mauritania protection. It was a pleasure to take care of them.

Soon Christmas 1992 and New Year 1993 arrived. MSF headquarters surprised us by sending a plane full of goodies on New Year's Eve. After a delicious special MSF dinner, we spent New Years' Eve and the beginning of 1993 New Year's Day listening to music and looking at the stars.

One simple food we were all missing a lot was salad. After 3 months in the desert, we were all dreaming about eating a fresh green salad with oil and vinegar. That's when Florence, one of my nurses went to the local market one Saturday morning and to her astonishment, found what she had been dreaming of for months. A local lady was selling 2 fresh green salads. Florence couldn't resist and bought the 2 of them. As she brought them back to the MSF house, everybody started salivating. We did have olive oil and vinegar. It would be a delight. Florence washed the salad, mixed it with oil and vinegar and put it on the table. Every body started grabbing some. I reminded everybody that it was too dangerous for us to eat local uncooked food. We could all become really sick. Nobody listened. Florence ate a whole bunch of salad, commenting on how good it tasted. Everybody else ate a little of it. I started salivating. I was dying to have some fresh salad. I hadn't had any for 3 months. My whole body told me to have some but my mind prevented me to do so. It was just too dangerous. My stomach ached with envy but I resisted. I ate my usual rice instead. Pretty soon, the salad bowl was empty. I was relieved.

I didn't wait too long for the consequences of the fresh salad. The following night, Florence started to have severe abdominal pain and diarrhea. Soon afterwards, everybody became sick, everybody but me. It only lasted a few hours for everybody except for Florence. She became so sick and so much in pain that she had to be transported to Nouakchott for urgent care. She paid a very high price for her fresh salad. It was a good lesson. It should be a good lesson for everybody who reads this book. If you travel to Africa, do not, I repeat, do not eat any local uncooked food bought in a local rural market, especially salads and vegetables. Do not eat any non peeled fruit. As for water, the only water you can drink is sealed bottled water, boiled water or water disinfected with chlorine tablets. If you are given bottled water, make sure you have to break a seal to open it and that it isn't tap water or dirty well water that was put in a used bottle. Otherwise, be ready to pay a high price …

Atar, my baby sheep, was growing fast and pretty soon he was of adult size. Unfortunately, before I knew it, we were in March 1993. It was the end of my mission. The hardest part for me was to separate from Atar. I left him with the physician who took over my work, hoping that that physician would take care of him and not roast him.

I wasn't ready to head back to Paris just yet. I decided to spend 2 weeks in the nearby Senegal before heading back to Paris. I was in Senegal when my parents gave me the bad news. A tumor had been found in my Dad's liver. It was most likely a metastasis from his colon cancer. His gastroenterologist had suggested a new treatment which was injection of alcohol directly in the tumor without anesthesia. Dad had decided to start the treatment which was extremely painful. Unfortunately, despite several injections, the tumor was growing rapidly. His gastroenterologist was telling him there was no other treatment. He had to continue. Was it a medical mistake again? There had to be other treatments. I had to get involved. I flew back to Paris.

Working for Doctors Without Borders in
Mauritania (I am on the extreme left)

With my baby sheep in my arms in Mauritania

# Chapter 12
## Trying to save Dad again

The following week, I was in Paris again. Dad had an alcohol treatment and he asked me to go with him. I saw him getting on the table. The radiologist located the tumor with an ultrasound machine. It was a large tumor, larger than I expected. It was 7 cm diameter (almost 3 inches). He filled up his syringe with pure alcohol and inserted the needle in the liver then in the tumor. As he started injecting alcohol, I heard Dad scream with intense pain. The injection seemed to last forever. Dad's unbearable scream was a torture to my ears. When the procedure was over, I took Dad home telling him this was the last time he was doing this. Not only was it extremely painful but it was doing nothing. The tumor was 4 cm diameter 2 months ago and now, it was 7 cm. It was not worth continuing. At this rate, he was going to die quickly. Dad said he was doing this treatment because it was the only one available. I told him I would explore other options.

Again, after taking care of people in a refugee camp, Dad became my special and only patient. The following 3 weeks, I went to Grand Rounds of every oncology and surgery department of every hospital in Paris. Each time, I presented Dad's case, showing all the CT scans and ultrasounds. Each time, I got a different answer. In one hospital, the medical team recommended to start chemotherapy. According to them, chemo could prolong his life 6 months. They recommended a certain protocol. In another one, they recommended another chemo cocktail saying that could prolong his life 8 months. In a third one, they said there was nothing to do. They all were against alcohol injections which had proven to be ineffective in liver metastasis. Each night at the dinner table, I would tell my parents about the result of searching. After 2 weeks, I got very discouraged.

On the 3rd week, I presented the case to Villejuif Cancer Center. There at Grand Rounds, to my surprise, the surgeon said he could remove the whole right lobe of Dad's liver. He said this was a very new technique that only *he* was doing. He had good results when the tumor was unique. This was Dad's case. The operation was risky but it was worth it because it could give a 5 year survival and some patients could even be cured. He suggested to start with 3 rounds of chemotherapy to start shrinking the tumor then surgery removing the right liver lobe (hoping the left lobe would be large enough to sustain life), then chemotherapy again to finish the job.

After everything I had heard before from all the other Grand Rounds, this seemed to be the best option. I was very enthusiastic when I went back home and talked to Dad about it. He said he trusted me and would do anything I thought would be right for him.

One week later we were at Villejuif Hospital in the surgeon's office.

Two weeks later, Dad had his first chemo treatment. I thought it would be somewhat easy. It was not.

The first round of chemotherapy was dreadful. Dad was so sick that he refused to have any more chemo. He wanted surgery right away. I tried to convince him to get 2 additional rounds. I couldn't. The result of the first round was great on the tumor. It shrunk well. We had to continue 2 more rounds. I had to convince Dad. I tried and tried but he still refused.

Disappointed, I went to see the surgeon who suggested to embolize the tumor to make it shrink some more. When I went back home to tell Dad, he accepted.

The embolization was a success and the tumor shrank some more. It was time to operate and do a right hepatectomy, risky surgery. We didn't know if Dad's left liver would be big enough to allow him to live. It was a risk we had to take. We took it.

The surgery went well despite the fact that Dad lost a lot of blood. He came out of surgery very anemic with a left liver barely big enough to sustain life. But the main thing was that he was still alive and the cancerous tumor was gone. It was a success. Dad's recovery was very slow in the hospital; he was so anemic that he was short of breath. He was still losing blood from the drain tubes. As his hemoglobin level was getting dangerously low and he was getting more and more short of breath, I had to intervene and demand that he received a blood transfusion. After the blood transfusion, Dad got better and started heading towards recovery quickly. Oh what a relief!!! I went to the hospital every day to see him, double check his blood results and the medications he was receiving and make sure he had everything he needed. During that time, Mom stayed home (hospital allergy) and was my emotional support and wonderful cook. One Sunday afternoon, I took him home for a few hours. Mom and he were ecstatic. Shortly after, I asked the surgeon if I could continue his care at home. He accepted. Dad being home, everything was simpler. I was checking his wound and changing his dressing everyday. Mom was cooking and everybody was happy. Our little family was together again.

One month later, we did another abdomen CT scan. To my amazement, Dad's liver had grown back almost completely and he was tumor free. That's when I learned that the liver is an organ that can grow very quickly at any age if resected. I didn't know that before or maybe I had forgotten.

After surgery, Dad refused to have chemotherapy. I didn't insist. He was doing well and was appreciating being alive tremendously.

That's when Dad and I started to go on long walks together and have long talks.

"Chris" he told me "I have something very special to ask you and I want you to promise me something"

Me: "Dad, you know I'll do anything and everything for you. You can ask anything you want".

Dad: "I know I am going to die soon. Eventually the cancer will grow again and kill me. I don't want to have ANY pain whatsoever. You know I don't take pain well. If I do start having pain and there is nothing to do to cure me any more, I want you to end my life. We are both doctors. We both know this is possible. I see no reason for me to agonize until death comes. You need to promise me you will end my life quickly if that time comes."

I was in shock. Yet, I did understand his demand very well. It was true that his cancer was very likely to metastasize again. In which part of his body would it go next? To his bones and make him suffer tremendously until death? To his lungs and make him short of breath more and more until death? The future was scary. Yet, it was illegal to practice euthanasia in France. How would we handle the situation? An idea came to my mind. I said: "Dad, you know it is illegal to practice euthanasia in France but what you could do is get a large amount of morphine tablets. If the time comes when your cancer is so advanced and so painful that you want to end your life, you can take that large amount of morphine. This way your life will end in peace and it won't be illegal"

Dad: "That's a good idea. I'll get some morphine. When I believe that that time has come, I'll call you. You can then confirm that there is nothing more to do and that the time is right. Only then will I take the morphine with you and your Mom near me to accompany me to the Other Side. Is that O.K. with you? Can you promise me you'll come when I call you?"

Me: "Yes Dad, that's O.K. with me. I promise that I'll come when you call me."

Dad: "You have to promise me one more thing"

Me: "What, Dad?"

Dad: "You have to promise to always make sure your Mom is O.K. She will be completely lost without me. She will need you. Promise me you will never let her down, you will always protect her and make sure she has everything she needs, promise me you'll take good care of her."

Me: "I promise, Dad, I'll never let her down and always take good care of her".

After that memorable talk, Dad felt much better. He started joking again and became his old self again. I knew that was because he wasn't too worried about the future any more. He had seen so many patients suffering till death. Morphine was given to them to ease their suffering but only in small quantities. They still remained in intense pain despite the morphine. A larger quantity would kill them which was against the law. This was a painful situation to be in and to watch. This would never happen to Dad.

# Chapter 13
# Working on a cruise ship

In October 1993, as Dad was getting better and stronger, I contacted Club Med again. I knew Dad's cancer would most likely come back and metastasize again but I was hoping he would have a few months of happiness before that. The Club Med recruiter told me she needed a physician to be on board the Club Med 2 cruise ship for 4 months. I was thrilled and ready to go.

The ship was at port in New Caledonia (near Australia) and was going to sail around the Vanuatu Islands for one cruise per week for 4 months. I would be the only physician on board, therefore on call 24 hours per day and I would have only one Japanese nurse to help me, also on call 24 hours. I would have a whole hospital on board with a defibrillator, X-Ray machine operating table and 2 hospital rooms with 2 beds in each one. That was more responsibility than I was used to. What would I do if we were at sea and a passenger had a heart attack? What if somebody else had an acute appendicitis and needed surgery right away? Would I have sterile instruments to perform an appendectomy? Would I have an anesthesiologist on board? The recruiter told me not to worry. I would have access to the main radio, and from New Caledonia a helicopter would come to pick up the patient. I felt somewhat reassured. Within minutes, my excitement took over. I would be the ship Doctor! This was too good to be true!

The following week I boarded a plane that flew me to Noumea, New Caledonia with two stop-overs in London, England and Sydney,

Australia. From Paris, it took me 29 hours to get to New Caledonia. It was a very long yet fantastic trip. At my arrival in Noumea, a taxi took me to the ship. I was astonished to see her beauty. She was a over 600 feet long, gorgeous, classy 5 masted vessel with 26,000 square feet of seven beautiful white sails. She could carry 392 passengers and 214 crew members. As I climbed on board, I let everybody know that I was the new physician. I was welcomed by all the GO's. One of them gave me a tour of the ship. I had never been on board a ship this large. She had 2 large spacious dining rooms, an exercise room, 2 swimming pools, a casino, 2 bars and a night club. I was struck by the size of each room. The bedrooms were spacious and clean. I was in awe.

The GO who gave me the tour, took me to my room which was completely at the bottom floor at the back of the ship. It was strategically located close to the nurse's station and to my hospital. She introduced me to my Japanese nurse, Kimi and left. Kimi and I started talking and soon found out that we were very different. She was typically Japanese and shy and I was typically French and more outspoken. Later, I understood why she had to be Japanese. You see, a lot of the tourists on board were Japanese and did not speak any other language. New Caledonia and the Vanuatu Islands were a very popular destination for Japanese honeymooners and Japanese couples in general. I would have to learn some medical Japanese terms. I would also have to learn how to operate an X-Ray machine. I had never before taken X-Rays myself. Kimi didn't know how to take X-Rays either. Together, we looked at the manual that came with the X-Ray machine and started studying it. Together, we did an inventory of all the drugs we had. I was happily surprised. We had just about everything we could need and were ready for almost any emergency. We then went on the deck were she introduced me to all the other GOs. Shortly after, I was introduced to the Captain of the ship who invited me to visit the bridge. I was one of the few people who were welcome anytime I wanted to be on the bridge.

A few hours later, the passengers started to board. Not surprisingly, at least 50% were Japanese. The rest were French and Australian tourists and a few Americans. Pretty soon I learned the routine. Everyday, around 6:00 pm, the ship would depart and we would sail the whole night, arriving in a different island everyday around 7:00am. What I had forgotten, was that I had a tendency to seasickness. Again, I had never been on a big ship but I was familiar to sailing small sailboats. I always got seasick on sailboats unless I was at the wheel. Then, I would stop being seasick. Well, forget about asking to be behind the wheel on this big ship. I had to find a way not to be sick. As we departed that first evening, the ship started rolling from right to left and tourists started running towards Kimi and I, throwing up. Within a few minutes, Kimi started throwing up too. Well, here we go, I said to myself, my one and only nurse is seasick! I cannot afford to be sick too, I have to take care of all those people. I quickly gave everybody some anti-seasickness patches to place behind their ears. I placed one under Kimi's ear too. When everybody got taken care of, I went to my bedroom and lay down on my bed. That's when I realized that I was extremely lucky. My bedroom, as I said before was at the bottom floor of the ship and at the back of it which was probably the most stable room in the whole ship. I could hardly feel the ship roll when I was in it. I looked at the window. All I could see was water spinning just like if I was looking at inside a washing machine. Yes, definitely, it was probably the worse view of all the rooms but the best one in terms of balance. I was thankful. The people who paid a lot of money to have a room on the top floor with beautiful views were probably swinging from right to left and back and forth a whole lot more than I was from my washing machine view.

As days went by, I became more and more at ease with my new status. I dressed all in white, white shirt, white pants, white cap, golden belt with a golden ship engraved in it. I became very popular. Remember the TV show "The Love Boat"? I became as popular as that doctor on the Love Boat. Each week, we had a new set of tourists arriving and a lot of single men would try to get close to me. I was also very popular among the GOs. Several GOs started courting me. The captain of the ship tried too. It was fun and I was enjoying being courted by all the men. The captain let me operate the ship whenever I wanted to, under his close supervision of course. All the guys would do me favors in hope that I would fall in love with them. I had a really great time.

Meals were unbelievable with buffets all the time. Since we had so many Japanese tourists, we also had several chefs. Among them was a Japanese chef who was creating delicious Japanese food. This soon became my favorite food on board.

The first week, I stayed on board the ship most of the time, enjoying the views from the ship. One of my favorite places to anchor was Hienghene bay in the North area of New Caledonia. The view was spectacular, anchored between two small islands made with rocks the first one looking like a sphinx, the second one looking like a chicken. We were the only ship in the bay, beautiful, white and majestic surrounded by mountains. We would then sail South East towards Pine Island, a beautiful small island just South East of New Caledonia, take the Havannah Pass to arrive in Noumea.

The second week I started exploring all the different Vanuatu Islands. I was stunned by their beauty. The water was so clear that you could see all the fish at the bottom just like in an aquarium. On Espiritu Santo Island and Pentecost Island, we were welcomed with a freshly cut coconut and a straw to suck out the delicious sweet refreshing coconut water. I also participated to all the activities, waterskiing, windsurfing, swimming etc..,

One of my most spectacular memories was climbing on top of the active volcano on Tanna Island. There were numerous explosions. The volcano was throwing stones and ashes up. Lava bombs were thrown 60 to 1000 feet up in the air. It was very loud and very scary. I had the video camera I had bought in St Martin and filmed everything. What if suddenly the volcano started throwing bigger lava bombs in my direction? What if liquid lava was shot out of it? Those thoughts flashed through my mind but didn't stay long. I was still fearless and young.

The second most memorable day was when we were at dock in Noumea and had a hurricane warning. I wasn't scared after the missed hurricane in Sandpiper, Florida. I decided to go for a long walk along the beach. I was walking when the winds became stronger and stronger. Within 15 minutes, I couldn't go forward any more. The winds were too strong. They were pushing me backwards. Palm trees started swinging dangerously and a heavy rain poured on me. When I realized I couldn't fight the winds which were getting louder and louder and I couldn't walk forward anymore, I became frightened and looked for a shelter. I tried running sideways. The winds were too strong, I couldn't even go sideways. Suddenly, behind me to the left, I saw a small building which I managed to reach. That's when, with my eyes astonished and wide opened, I witnessed the incredible power of nature. I was close to the eye of a hurricane for the first time of my life. It was exciting! It was empowering! I was young and thought I was invincible. The fear only stayed with me a few minutes then awe took over. I was discovering the world. I was discovering the strength of nature. Palm trees were bending almost to their breaking point. Parts of roofs were flying away. Large leaves and wood pieces were in constant motion in the air. I stayed there several hours in awe then the winds weakened.

I was extremely lucky that the eye of the hurricane never went over Noumea. I was also extremely lucky because in the 4 months of my assignment as the ship physician, I never had any serious life threatening emergency to address. I later heard that the physician that came after me had to deal with a lot of deadly emergencies. His 4 months were very hard whereas mine were very pleasurable.

As my contract was finishing, I arranged to stay 2 weeks longer in the area and decided to go to Sidney, Australia. I had met a few Australian tourists who had invited me to stay at their house in Sidney. After all, I was so close to Australia, It was worth taking the opportunity to visit it. I was wondering if maybe I would like to live in Australia. I knew that I couldn't live in Paris for the rest of my life. I knew I would love to live in California. But what about Australia? It was worth exploring.

Well, I spent 2 weeks in Sidney and loved it. I loved Australia but I decided I wasn't born to live there. It was time to fly back to Paris to check on my Dad and get ready for a new destination.

Since Dad's health was good, I called the Club Med recruiter. Club Med needed a physician to fly to Greece. I unpacked and immediately repacked. The new resort was Gregolimano on Evia Island, near the Aegean Sea, 150 kilometers North of Athens. Usually that resort had no significant medical problems and didn't need a full-time physician. Well that year, it was different. The island was infested by bees. Thousands of bees were flying around tourists during meals which were outside. Some people were allergic to bee stings and for them a bee sting could be fatal. I had to be on site with injectable epinephrine and steroids just in case someone had a problem. It would be a short contract. There was only one month left for prime tourist season.

As I arrived in Athens, I was surprised by the beauty of Greece. This was my first time there and I was in awe again. When I arrived on the Island of Evia, I couldn't stop admiring the stunning views. I arrived late at Gregolimano that day. After one good night of sleep, as I was heading for the breakfast buffet, I noticed some bees. They became more numerous as I got closer and closer to the buffet. Then I became completely horrified. They were thousands of bees flying everywhere around the buffet and every breakfast table. Tourists were surrounded by them. I started understanding why I had to be on site. Surprisingly enough, nobody was getting stung. I could relax. The first 2 weeks, everything went well. Tourists were doing great, not complaining too much about the bees still hovering around their tables at each meal. Bees were behaving themselves, staying interested in food and not landing on human skin. I was enjoying Greek food and the different activities of the resort when suddenly I heard somebody scream. It was a young 16 year old girl. She had opened her mouth to eat a bite of omelet when a bee entered her mouth and bit her on the tongue. I took care of her right away. Fortunately she wasn't allergic to bee stings. I made sure the stinger was out of her tongue, kept her in the nurse's station one hour and let her go with a simple anti inflammatory treatment. One more week went by without any significant event. I thought everything would go well until the rest of the month when *it* happened. That was my worse fear. I was hoping *it* would not happen but *it* did.

Suddenly, at breakfast, a 220 lbs, 6' 4" muscular 24 year old man was stung by a tiny bee. Within seconds, he collapsed. It was so spectacular seeing how much damage a tiny bee could do to a strong, muscular, healthy, young man. Within seconds, I was injecting him with epinephrine. We transported him to the infirmary only to find that his blood pressure was 70 over palp. He could hardly talk. I injected him with IV steroids and IV epinephrine again. His blood pressure went back up and he started talking to us again but it didn't last long. He went into shock again and within seconds, I couldn't get a blood pressure any more. I continued injecting IV epinephrine and IV steroids until his blood pressure came back up. Half an hour later, his blood pressure was back to normal and he was talking to us again. I kept him in the infirmary a few more hours. When I was sure he was stable enough to go back to his room, we let him go. My nurse and I sighed with relief. We almost lost him. It was lucky we were right next to him within seconds when the sting happened, otherwise he might not have survived. The following day, he came by the infirmary to thank us deeply. We did indeed save his life. He would have to carry an epinephrine pen with him at all times now. He was definitely allergic to bee venom. No other accident or incident happened during the rest of my stay and pretty soon it was time to fly back home. I visited the gorgeous Delphes ruins before leaving Greece and headed to the airport.

As we took off for Paris, I was thinking how fragile we could be. One day, we could be this strong healthy body and the following day, we could be dead, just like that, with no warning. I thought about my parents. What if they were going to disappear soon? Would I remember their voice? Would I remember how their bodies were? Would I remember how they used to tell me bedtime stories? Would I remember their advice? The answer was clearly no, no and no. I had to fix that. I was carrying with me a video camera. It was time to film my parents. It was time to engrave them in my mind and in film for the many years ahead.

When I arrived at the Charles de Gaulle airport, I took the RER again to Bourg-La-Reine. I always loved taking this RER. It was taking me all through Paris and reminding me where I grew up. As I arrived at my parents' house, I hugged them for a long time. I was happy to see them again. I was happy to see that Dad was still in great shape. I told them how much I loved them both and they told me how much they loved me. I knew Dad's health would not hold on for very much longer. I told them about my idea to film them for the posterity. They agreed.

The following day, I spent the whole day filming them. I asked Dad to tell me stories about his childhood. I asked him to tell me advice to help me live the rest of my life. I asked Mom to tell me some bedtime stories, the ones she used to tell me when I was a child and couldn't get to sleep. I asked her to tell me stories about her childhood and then I asked her to tell me her advice for the rest of my life. I got everything on tape. I also filmed them interacting with each other, laughing and holding hands. This tape is the best thing I did. It is one of the most precious things I own. How many people can watch their parents telling stories, joking and giving us advice? Not many people think about making such a tape. When your parents are alive and healthy, you don't need such a tape. When they are dead, you wish you had it, but it is too late. I would strongly recommend that everyone make such a tape. It is priceless. Now that my Dad is dead, I watch him from time to time. This way, the memory of his voice, his body language, his strength, his intelligence and his love remain sharp in my heart and in my mind. When I think my memories are fading, I watch the tape over and over again. My mother is still with us but I know the time will come when she will leave me too. Fortunately this tape of her will remain live in my heart too and when I'll be 80 years old myself, I know I will enjoy watching her and listen to her telling me a bedtime story. It will bring me Peace.

# Chapter 14
## Dad's cancer is back

The following year, in the middle of the summer when most physicians are on vacation, Dad had a recurrence of his cancer. There was a new tumor in his liver. This time it was on the top part of the liver and was extending to the right lung. This was bad.

I tried to contact the surgeon who had operated on him the first time but unfortunately he was on vacation. This was a very unlucky timing. In France, you don't want to have to go to a hospital in August. Everything stops in August in Paris because most of the French population in on vacation. The few businesses that don't want to take their vacation in August still end up doing so because they don't have customers any more. So, they might as well close. August is the month when Paris belongs to tourists. Parisians are at the seaside, tourists are in Paris.

Well, here we were August 1st with a liver cancer extending to the lung that needed to be resected urgently. This was not a procedure that just any surgeon could do successfully. Only a few surgeons in the world were skilled enough and experienced enough to do it. The surgeon we knew had just left for his annual vacation. We had to wait until September. In the meantime, we had to start chemotherapy again.

Dad hated chemotherapy. Some people don't take it too badly. He was not one of those. For him, it was bad, really bad. He was terribly nauseous and tired for a week following each round. He had a very hard time handling being sick and being in pain.

As soon as his surgeon returned from vacation in September, I contacted him. He agreed to operate Dad the following week. I was so thankful! That time, I decided not to be in the operating room. Being in the OR at the time of Dad's surgery was becoming emotionally harder and harder each time for me. The following week, I let Dad go to the OR by himself. That proved to be a bad decision. The surgery itself went well but when Dad woke up, he couldn't move his right foot any more. I felt guilty. Usually, each time Dad went to the operating room, I was with him, covering him with a blanket if he was too cold and positioning his arms, legs and head the right way so that he wouldn't get any cramps. This time I wasn't there, the surgeon had placed his legs against an iron bar pressing on his fibula bilaterally. Dad had stayed like this for several hours during the surgery. On the right side, the iron bar had pressed and injured his commun peroneal nerve. This had paralyzed his right foot which he couldn't lift up any more. He had a post-traumatic dropped foot and had a hard time walking. It took several months for the nerve to recover. Had I been in the OR this wouldn't have happened. I decided to be in the O.R. with him each time in the future, no matter how emotionally hard it was for me. Dad's wellbeing was more important than my emotions.

As Dad was still having trouble walking, unfortunately, his cancer markers went up. He needed chemotherapy long term if he wanted to continue living. He then started a long ordeal of chemotherapy cocktails every 3 weeks. This was very hard on him since chemo was making him sick but he wanted to fight his cancer as much as possible to be with my Mom as long as possible. My parents after 45 years of marriage were still very much in love. I don't think I heard them fight once. They were made for each other and were a great example of the Perfect Love.

# Chapter 15
# Searching for Mr. Perfect

The following year, I decided I had enough of traveling. The last 5 years, I had traveled almost nonstop for work. It was time for me to stop and settle down. But where? I certainly didn't want to settle down in France. Even though I was born and raised there, it didn't feel like I belonged there. I hated the fact that people were smoking everywhere in public places. I hated working in France. I was more attracted to foreign men than to French men.

During all my travels, I had thought about settling down in Australia but Australia didn't feel right either. I had thought about Norway, Sweden, China and Japan. None of those felt right. The USA on the other hand felt right. I remembered that my dream when I was 13 years old was to become an actress and live in Los Angeles. I had traveled to California and noticed that in Los Angeles, I felt home so much that each time, it was physically and emotionally painful to leave. I was very much attracted to American men and as soon as they were speaking a few words of American, I was charmed. It sounded like music to my ears. I had learned British English at school but always had a hard time understanding British people. American language on the other hand, I understood immediately. I decided I would settle down in Los Angeles.

When I bought my plane ticket to Los Angeles, I felt my whole body shivering with pleasure.

In Los Angeles, my new goal was to find my Prince Charming. I was finally ready! I had done all the traveling, all the exploring I wanted in my life. I was finally ready for that special and perfect Prince Charming I had always been told about. I knew deep in my heart there was somebody out there especially for me. But how could I find him?

The problem is that nobody teaches us how to find a mate. School teachers teach us history, geography, mathematics, etc which allows us to be successful in business. But how can we be successful in our family life? Isn't that as important as having a great career? If we do manage to have a harmonious marriage, we can raise our kids in that great environment and they, when it becomes their turn, will have much more chance to find the right mate. But how can we find a mate? Who can teach us? Only somebody who knows can teach us but who knows? That's a good question. Most people don't know. Most people have chosen all their life the wrong persons for them and they still haven't learned. Our parents, if they know, should teach us but do they really know? Most don't. Most don't have the perfect marriage or are divorced. Most don't have the first clue how to find the right mate.

Here is what I had learned at this point of my life. Finding the right mate seems very easy and simple but in fact, it is very difficult and complex. Yes, you should be physically attracted to the person but this cannot be the only reason to be together. You should have some common goals. You should have compatible religions. You should be compatible in the kind of house and house decoration you want, in the number of children you want, in the way to raise your children. If opinions are different, you should be able to respect the other person's opinion. Emotionally, you should be able to connect with each other. Intellectually, you should be able to understand each other. Sexually, you should be compatible.

It is amazing to me to see how many people are sexually incompatible. For some people (like me), sex is a very important element in the marriage. For some other people, it isn't. Some people need to have sex only once a month. Some people need to have sex twice a day! Imagine if a woman who only enjoys sex once a month marries a man who needs it twice a day! It can be a disaster. Imagine a woman who needs a man inside of her for 20 minutes in order to have a vaginal orgasm marrying a man who ejaculates prematurely (i.e., ejaculating 5 to 60 seconds after penetration). Yes, there are drugs. Well, with drugs, we can manage to triple his length of time inside a woman. So, instead of 5 to 60 seconds, he can manage at his best to stay 3 minutes inside of her! When she needs 20 minutes, 3 minutes still isn't going to enable her to reach orgasm. She could be miserable! What about the man's size? Is it important? For some of us, it is. You see, some women will never have an orgasm. Some women will only have clitoral orgasms. For those, size is not that important. But for women (like me) who have clitoral and vaginal orgasms, size is extremely important. With the perfect size man, I have an average of 20 vaginal and clitoral orgasms each time I have sex. This brings me an inner deep pleasure that stays with me for several hours each time. It causes me to release endorphins. It influences my whole night and day. If my partner is too small, I don't feel anything. If my partner is too big, it hurts. You might think that all men and women are made the same, well they are not. Some men are very small even when erect. Other men are much larger than average. Some women have a short and narrow vagina. Others have a longer and wider vagina. Imagine a man with a large penis marrying a woman with a very small vagina? It could be a disaster! She will likely be in pain, if not now, maybe after 2 years of marriage. Now imagine a man with a very small penis marrying a woman with a large vagina! For sure this woman will have no orgasm after penetration. She will most likely not feel much! By the way, it will not be great for him either. For some women, it is not a problem because they never had any orgasm and therefore won't miss it. They might say "Honey, you want sex, no problem! Do you mind if I continue watching TV during that time…"? For other women, it could be horrible.

There are rare situations where a man's penis is slightly bent towards the right or the left or the front or the back. It must be compatible with the shape of the woman's vagina.

Occasionally, a woman's vagina will not tolerate the pH of the man's sperm. She might have recurring urinary tract infections or vaginal infections while her vagina will have no problem with another man's sperm. Imagine you love the man but your vagina hates his sperm! This could be another disaster!

That's why I could never understand why people would get married before having sex. In my opinion, it is taking a big gamble on life. I was not ready to take that gamble. Sex was too important for me. I know I am shocking a lot of people by writing this. I know it is religiously unacceptable to have sex before marriage but what if there are sexual incompatibilities? I guess it is OK for people to wait until marriage to have sex as long as they determine that sex doesn't have to be perfect and that they will accept and be thankful for whatever they'll discover.

Anyways, this was not my problem. My problem was to find men that would fit all my requirements. I wanted my Prince Charming to be educated, sensitive, Catholic, funny, muscular, tall, good-looking with blue eyes, non-smoker and with no children from a previous marriage. I needed him to be sexually compatible with me. So many requirements, you tell me! Well, yes! I was not young and inexperienced about life any more. I was much more mature and knew exactly the kind of man I wanted. The big question was: "Where do you find such a man"?

"Go to a video dating service" Richard, my best friend said "I know a friend of mine who met his wife this way. They are now married and are very happy." I had met Richard at a seminar in Big Sur 1 year prior and we had remained friends ever since. He was a teacher and had started teaching me all the basics of living in LA. He was wonderful and always very helpful. I thought the video dating idea was great. The following day, I explored a video dating service in West LA.

The dating service was a big place. It looked very nice and I immediately liked it. The lady at the desk managed to convince me that I could find the perfect man I was looking for. "Tall, strong, muscular, blue eyes, no children, doesn't smoke, highly educated, Catholic, sensitive, has a sense of humor and is a great lover? No problem, there are at least 300 men that fit the description!" She said. I shivered with excitement thinking in myself: "Really??? This cannot be possible. This would be a dream come true!!!" I signed up immediately with the service. Then, I spent the whole afternoon in the library, looking at profiles. The lady was right. There were quite a few men matching my requirements. Amazing! I got several binders with men's profiles and spend hours studying each profile and looking at the different videos. This became my full-time job. For the next 3 weeks, I spent 6 hours a day in that library selecting profiles that would match my dream. I selected one hundred of them!

On my 5th day of selecting profiles, I saw a very handsome man in his early forties, dressed in a business suit, approximately 5'9" coming in. I thought to myself "He looks nice but he is way too short and not muscular enough for me". The receptionist was trying to convince him to stay: "But sir, you just joined! You need to take advantage of the place and start looking at the books!" He said that he had no time for that but somehow she convinced him to stay a few minutes. I was amused by the scene. It was a nice and refreshing break. To my surprise the man grabbed a few books and sat at my table. I glanced at him. He had a very friendly face with beautiful blue eyes. He looked embarrassed. He glanced at the huge pile of books in front of me and seemed impressed. The expression of his face was so funny that it made me laugh. We started talking. His name was Steve. He was so nice and so funny! I felt immediately at ease with him, as if I had known him for years. A few minutes later, I went to the men's bookshelf to look at Steve's file while he went to the women's bookshelf to read my file. I was curious to know more about him. I liked what I read. He was 5 years older than me and had never been married. He was a computer engineer. We were definitely very compatible. He did fit all my requirements except for one. He wasn't tall enough.

As we each came back to our seats, he asked me if I had dinner yet. As I answered negatively, he asked me if I wanted to join him for dinner. I decided to accept. I was in mood for Chinese food. It turned out he loved Chinese food too so he took me to a close by Chinese restaurant. There I decided I would be completely honest with him. I had no time to play anymore. I was looking for "Mr. Perfect" and I needed to tell him. To his surprise, I completely opened up. I probably shocked him a lot. I told him that I was looking for "Mr. Perfect", that he wasn't tall enough for me but that he was definitely close. I told him I had a list of questions for all the candidates and that I wanted to practice on him. As food arrived, I started my questions. Steve was so surprised by them that he could hardly eat at the beginning. My questions were: What are your hobbies? Have you been married before? Do you smoke? What is your dream in life? Then came more personal questions: Do you have a hairy chest? How often in the week do you need to have sex? How long does it take you to have an orgasm? Steve answered all the questions while blushing a lot. He was clearly uncomfortable but was trying to be as honest as possible. His discomfort was so obvious that I started laughing. He asked me if I intended to ask those questions to all the men I was going to meet. My answer was "Yes, of course!" I told him I wanted to meet a lot of men.

The strangest thing happened. I started feeling so good with him. He was so easy to be with. If only I could find the same man in a taller version, it would be wonderful. That's exactly what I told him at the end of the dinner. He wished me luck and asked me for my phone number. He wanted to stay in touch, to be friends with me if anything and to keep track of my "shopping". I gave him my phone number.

The next few months of my "shopping" were fun. I met 50 men and started dating a few of them. Two of them were exactly what I was looking for. One thing was bothering me though. With none of them was I feeling as good as I was feeling with Steve. Steve kept calling me regularly. We started going to dinner once a month as friends. I would tell him everything. He was enjoying hearing about my difficult dates. He was having a hard time finding women to date. We were laughing a lot. I was feeling so incredibly good and could be completely myself with him. More and more often a question would pop in my mind. Could Steve be the one? I refused to consider this idea. The answer had to be no. I had to continue my search.

A few months later, I went back to Paris to check on my parents. When I came back, I stayed in a different place with a different phone number. I decided not to call Steve but to continue looking for "Mr. Perfect". I went back to the Video dating service and dated a few more men. A lot of them were very close to what I was looking for but I couldn't feel good with any of them. One day, as I was in the Video dating service library, I felt a tap on my shoulder. I looked up and saw Steve looking at me. "You are back! How are you?" I was shocked. I hadn't called him on purpose and here he was in front of me! Again, immediately I felt this disturbing feeling of being so at ease with him. I told him about my recent dating. He asked me for my new phone number. I gave it to him. I had to be completely honest with him. I told him I thought he was a wonderful man and he deserved to find somebody who would love him completely. I didn't love him the way he deserved to be loved. He had to start dating other women. When I was done talking, he told me his truth. He had fallen in love with me and thought I was the perfect woman for him. Nevertheless, he understood me and would start dating other women again. Again, we had this complete simple honesty and openness with each other which was astonishing for me. It felt good to be with him but I had to continue looking for Mr. Perfect.

One month later, a friend of mine introduced me to his best friend Mike. I fell in love with Mike and soon afterwards moved in with him. At that time, I called Steve to let him know that I had found Mr. Perfect and was moving in with him. He asked me how tall Mr. Perfect was and laughed when I said that Mr. Perfect was shorter than him and had brown eyes. He told me that he himself had started seriously dating a lady who was very interested in him. All was well then. We said goodbye and wished each other good luck.

I was so happy I had found Mike. Moving in with him was a big event in my life. His house was big and beautiful. It had a swimming pool and a large master bedroom. My first month with him was wonderful. The second month was not so good. The third month was terrible. The fourth month, I became very depressed. I didn't think I could live with any man. The very first man I had lived with was my first husband. That lasted 3 weeks. This second time, here I was in our 4th month of living together and it was a disaster. One day, I decided to drop by the video dating service again.

Guess who was there too? Steve was there! He had not been there for 4 months and the same day, had decided to drop by too. That was unbelievable! This was the 3rd time I was meeting him unexpectedly! May be there was a reason why I was meeting him for the 3rd time? One story came to my mind: A man was dying in the sea. A small fishing boat came by to rescue him. He refused saying he was waiting for God to rescue him. Then a cruise ship came to rescue him. He refused saying he was waiting for God to rescue him. Then a helicopter came to rescue him. Again he refused for the same reason. He then died and went to heaven. In heaven, he saw God and asked him "God, why didn't you rescue me? I was waiting for you to rescue me". God answered: "I did! I sent a fishing boat to rescue you but you refused, then I sent a cruise ship then I finally sent a helicopter but you refused all of those!"

Maybe God had sent me Steve twice already and each time, I had refused to recognize him. This was the 3rd time. Was I not seeing something I was supposed to see? I looked at Steve. After living with Mike who was shorter, Steve looked to me so much taller! It suddenly hit me! He was a really gorgeous man with his tidy suit and his beautiful blue eyes! I looked at him more closely. He looked very sad. We started talking. He told me that the woman he was seriously dating wanted a child from him. He was about to accept being the Dad. He didn't love her the way he loved me but she seemed to really care about him. He asked me about my living with Mike. I told him it was a disaster. I was really unhappy and was about to move out. I had the feeling it would be the last time God was sending Steve to me. I suddenly opened my eyes and realized he could be THE ONE. He could be my Prince Charming. I had never looked at him that way. Again, I told him my thoughts. I had always been open and honest with him. This was not about to change. Not now! He smiled and said: "I am happy you can open your eyes. I have been waiting for this Moment for a long time. I have known we were made for each other since the day I met you."

We decided to go for a walk. Steve took my hand. His hand was warm and strong. His touch felt so good! We remained silent for a while. I was deep in my thoughts. After 10 minutes, I asked Steve a question I would never have asked before: "Can I move in with you?" He looked very surprised, paused, seemed to think very deeply and answered "Yes, you can". Yes, I know, it was an outrageous question to ask especially being a good Catholic girl but at this point of my life, I couldn't care less. The 2 men I had tried to live with, including my first husband, had been complete disasters. I believed that I could spend week-ends with men but that I wasn't able to live with anybody. I didn't want to marry 10 different men only to find out that I couldn't live with any of them. Each time, the first few days were great and then things would deteriorate rapidly. Forget about marriage first and then move in. I knew this didn't work for me. That's what I explained to Steve.

Steve had said yes. He had never lived with any woman before. This was a big step for him. For me, it wasn't really a big step. I was afraid it would be another disaster. I told him about my fears. He told me not to worry. We would do our best and whatever happens would be fine. I thanked him. It felt so good to be with him.

Four days later, I moved into Steve's house in Torrance. It was a large and very pleasant 3 bedroom house with a 4 car garage. I had my own bedroom. He had his. We were friends not lovers. I was scared. Little by little, I started falling in love with him. That was not a light and superficial feeling. It was a deep, going deeper everyday feeling of care, admiration, respect and LOVE. It was what everybody was talking about! That special feeling I had never experienced before. Steve was very funny and we would laugh all the time together. He was very caring and helpful, wanting to do everything he could for me. He changed the living room furniture for me and ordering just the kind of furniture I really liked. He ordered a turquoise couch and recliner. My 2 favorite colors are turquoise and purple. Everything I buy has to be turquoise or purple or both colors together. Steve started buying me turquoise and purple things. It was wonderful. He could fix everything and anything. If I had a problem making anything work, he would open it, find the problem and fix it within the hour, sometimes within minutes. I was good at fixing medical problems. He was good at fixing everything else.

Within the first month, we started to be physically very close and soon after, I moved from my bedroom to his bedroom. I discovered that he had a very muscular and strong body. He had been raised on a farm and had phenomenal biceps. He was much taller than I had ever seen him. As for sex, it was wonderful. He was the perfect fit for me. He needed sex as often as me and as long as me. I started having my most intense orgasms ever. Unlike my usual pattern with men, the first month with Steve was wonderful, the second month was even more wonderful, and the third month more wonderful than the second and this was still getting better. When I thought it couldn't get any better, the following month was still better. I had my answer. Steve was the Prince Charming I had been looking for. I was created for him. He was created for me. I was in LOVE, real LOVE, not infatuation (and I knew the difference). We were making each other really blossom. We decided to get married. We set a date: October 26. I started looking for a dress, a church and a reception place. Steve started working on the honeymoon trip which was going to be in Maui, Hawaii.

I met his work colleagues who couldn't say enough compliments about him. He was working as a System Engineering Consultant for Digital Equipment Corporation and was known in the whole company and the companies related for his perfect work. He architected complex networks for large Government and Aerospace programs, most programs utilizing $10-30M in computer products and services. He had a breadth of knowledge on VAX/VMS, Alpha/VMS and UNIX systems, PCs and PC integration, and networking. Steve was definitely a perfectionist who would frequently work a whole night preparing for a presentation. As for proposals, he would stay up several nights in a row preparing for them. He was always praised for his high work quality and ethic. I was proud of being by his side.

We flew to Pennsylvania where Steve introduced me to his entire family. I was welcomed with open arms by everyone. I met his Dad Joe who looked so much like him just a little bit older. I met his Mom Martha who, despite being in her 60's, was young and cheerful at heart. They both had a great sense of humor and appeared to be a very happy couple. Steve had grown up on a farm in Southwestern Pennsylvania in a small town called Scenery Hill. It was beautiful there. Deer and wild turkeys often ran through the farm. Joe, Steve's Dad, had taught Steve to be self sufficient and to be able to fix anything- electrical, plumbing, wood, machinery, etc.…. They used to raise cows and chickens but had stopped farming many years prior. It was wonderful to meet Steve's parents. Martha cooked and baked for days before our arrival and served us the most wonderful meals. It was a pure pleasure to stay with them. I also met Steve's 2 wonderful and beautiful sisters with their respective husbands and 2 very handsome brothers with their wives. Here I was, coming from a very small family in Paris, transported to the middle of the Pennsylvania countryside in a very large family. It felt so different and yet so good. I also met my 2 future nieces and 5 future nephews. I immediately loved them. I was really happy.

Engagement with my future husband Steve

# Chapter 16
# Wedding or no wedding?

I called my parents to tell them about the wedding. They were thrilled. Dad was still in chemotherapy to prevent the cancer from spreading. But he had enough of it and wanted to stop. I asked him to continue until one month before the wedding. I wanted him to walk me down the aisle and appreciate his time in California with Mom. I was afraid that if he stopped his chemo earlier, his cancer would be too advanced for him to fly to LA.

He did exactly what I asked him to do. Painfully, he continued chemo until one month prior to my wedding. When he had completely recuperated his strength, he and Mom got ready to fly to LA. It was October 9th.

Life with Steve was wonderful. Each month, we were more and more in love. It was heavenly. Little did I know that things would suddenly change!

On October 9, Steve came to me with a look I had never seen before.

Steve: "Chris, I have given it a lot of thought and I feel I am not ready to marry you. We have to cancel the wedding."

I felt my heart melting. I almost fainted. It could only be a joke. It was 2 weeks before the wedding. I had spent so much time finding the right dress, the right church, the right reception place, the right DJ. I had ordered all the meals, the flowers and the music. Steve had come with me to talk to the priest who was going to marry us. He liked him, he liked the church, he liked the reception place and he liked the DJ. We had been living together for one year and things were wonderful. I had been working on the wedding for the last 6 months. I had organized Dad's chemotherapy so that he could fly to LA. I looked at the time. It was 7.00 am Paris time and my parents were probably as we were speaking getting ready to leave the house to go to the airport. It was really bad timing. If Steve didn't want to get married, why didn't he say so earlier? I couldn't understand life any more. It had to be a joke.

Me: "Steve, is it a joke? You don't really mean this, do you?"

Steve, looking at me with a really dark look that I had never seen before: "No, unfortunately, it is not a joke. I don't want to get married. You can continue living with me but we have to cancel the wedding"

Me: "My parents are about to leave the house right now to go to the airport. Should I call them to tell them not to come?"

Steve: "Yes, you should call them"

My heart broke! So, it was really not a joke! Steve wanted to cancel everything! I fell into deep darkness and tears started pouring out of my eyes. I tried calming down. I had to call my parents.

Me: "O.K., I'll call them but you will have to talk to my Dad to explain the situation"

Steve: "I'll talk to your Dad"

We called my parents. I told them the wedding was cancelled. Steve talked to my Dad in English (my Dad was speaking English fluently). They were just about to leave the house. The phone conversation was short and left them in shock. They cancelled their flight.

I was devastated. All my dreams had suddenly collapsed. Steve was suggesting I could stay living with him. He said he still loved me but didn't want to marry me yet. Maybe later in the future? When I asked when, he said he didn't know. In how many years? He didn't know. When we went to bed that day, I couldn't make love to him. I couldn't even sleep in the same bedroom. I went for a walk. When I came back, I made the bed in the guest bedroom again. After a sleepless night, my decision was made. I told Steve that after what had happened I couldn't stay with him any more. I had to move out. I gave him back his engagement ring and started looking for a place to stay. I found a place available and decided to move in 3 days. I started packing. All the framed paintings on the walls were mine, painted by my Mom. I took them all out of their hooks. All the walls in the living room and bedrooms looked baren. I couldn't stop crying. All my dreams were gone. I would have to start from scratch again. I had to be strong.

The following 2 days were dreadful. I was crying all the time, making phone calls to organize my moving out. I was still living with Steve but we were just friends now. We didn't talk much. Everything had been said. He tried to convince me to stay living with him but he rapidly saw that it wasn't possible. Canceling the wedding was a huge shock for me, probably much more than Steve had expected. I was not well. I couldn't eat any more. I started losing a lot of weight. I was very depressed. I had to move out.

On the evening of the 2nd day, as I was ready to move out the following morning, Steve went for a long walk outside. He came back late at night. He then knocked on the door of my bedroom and woke me up, handing me a little jewelry box.

Steve: "Chris, I love you. Will you marry me?"

I jumped up: "Steve, what are you saying? You don't want to marry me, remember? The wedding is cancelled! I am moving out!"

Steve: "I don't want you to move out. We are made for each other. I'll be miserable without you and I see you'll be miserable too. I made a huge mistake. I was just really scared. Please forgive me and please accept to marry me."

I couldn't believe my ears. Was I dreaming? I tried pinching myself. It hurt. It wasn't a dream! It was reality!

Me: "Steve, when do you want to get married?"

I was expecting an answer like in one year or 2 years but he said: "If it is still possible I would like to get married as planned - in less than 2 weeks".

I was in disbelief: "It might be still possible but I want you to be sure. I won't be able to go through something like this many times otherwise I am going to have a heart attack and I am going to give my Dad a heart attack too."

Steve: "I am sure. I won't ask you to cancel any more. Will you marry me?"

He looked so genuinely sorry and I still loved him so much. I fell in his arms and said: "Yes, I will marry you".

The following day, instead of moving out, I put all my paintings back on all the walls and I called the church and the reception place again. Both places were still available for the same dates. The wedding could still happen as originally planned. I called my parents again and had Steve talk to my Dad again, apologizing to him. My parents couldn't believe their ears. My Dad asked him if he was really sure of his decision this time. Steve said he was sure. They decided to take the next available flight to LA. I was happy again and singing again. I decided not to be sexually intimate with Steve until after the wedding. The wedding night would be a real exciting wedding night. But would the wedding really happen? Would Steve say "yes" in front of the priest? I wasn't sure…

I had chosen Richard my best friend and Christine who was a physician from Romania studying to become licensed in the States to be in my wedding. Christine would be my maid of honor and Richard would light the candles and escort everyone.

The day of the wedding came quickly. As I was waking up, I immediately went to the window to look at the color of the sky. It was blue with bright sunshine. I was immediately relieved. The wedding rehearsal was 20 hours before and the weather was so bad and stormy that the power was out at the Neighborhood church. We had to do the rehearsal by candle-light. Maybe it was more romantic that way but the storm had been very scary. Fortunately, the storm was gone and the weather was beautiful.

I went to have my hair and make-up professionally done then I put on my gorgeous wedding dress. It had lace and pearls everywhere. I looked so beautiful in it! I was so excited! Steve's parents, brothers and sisters had arrived the previous day. My parents were there. Everything was ready, flowers, church ceremony, reception and dance. I was so happy. I only had one question in my mind, though. Would Steve say "I do"? As the photographer was finishing taking pictures and everybody was taking their seats in the church, I became very worried. Nobody had seen Steve yet. He hadn't arrived. As I started telling how worried I was to my parents, my mother proceeded to tell me how my father was also late for his own wedding. My father told me not to worry. Steve had promised him that everything would go well. Despite his words of reassurance, I started worrying more and more. Maybe Steve got second thoughts. Maybe he had decided not to come. As I was imagining all the worse scenarios, I suddenly heard people applauding. Steve had arrived. I was relieved. He was just late as he usually tended to be. The church ceremony started.

As Steve was with Tom his best friend and best man near the priest, my special music played and I started walking slowly down the aisle. I had my Mom on one side and my Dad on my other side, my 2 beautiful nieces Alisha and Sarra both of them 4 years old behind me carrying the back of my dress. Everybody was looking at me. I was walking slowly towards Steve. It was the most beautiful day of my life. My eyes started shedding tears from all the emotion. Steve was looking at me with love and awe. At that time only, I knew that the wedding was going to happen. As we exchanged our vows and our rings, I almost fainted. My emotion was very intense. Soon afterwards, we were declared husband and wife. I stayed in my husband's arms kissing him for a long time. Everybody congratulated us. The after wedding pictures took place at the seaside at the back of the church. The reception and dance went extremely well and the following day, we were off to Maui for our honeymoon.

Maui was fabulous. Steve had reserved an incredible ocean front room in an awesome hotel on Kanaapali shore. We spent our honeymoon snorkeling with spotted eagle rays, playing tennis, bicycling down Haleakala volcano, taking helicopter rides, eating delicious meals, drinking superb wines and loving each other. It was a real honeymoon like those you see in movies. It was so romantic and so perfect! We were so much in love with each other!

When we came back from Maui, we heard that Richard my best friend and Christine my maid of honor had fallen in love with each other. I was thrilled.

As for Steve and I, our life as husband and wife started. I was afraid it would be different. I was afraid something would happen at 3 weeks but nothing did. Steve was the most loving husband. He knew about my fears and did everything he could to make me happy. He succeeded beautifully. At 3 weeks of marriage, I was the happiest wife on this planet. At one month, 2, 3, 4, 5 months of marriage, I was still the happiest wife on this planet. I decided to celebrate our anniversary each month for the first year. After 10 years of marriage, I was still the happiest wife on the planet, married to the most wonderful man on earth. As for Richard and Christine, they got married one year after us and remain to this day my best friends.

I didn't think that sex could get any better than it was but it did. We discovered new love making positions. I started to have one extremely intense orgasm per minute and could have 20 or more orgasms each time we had sex. What a blast! Nothing else in life can compare to an intense, deep, overpowering golden shower of orgasms. It was pure heaven, heaven that made me wake up with a smile and made every day a very beautiful one.

We could talk for hours and talked about everything. Steve was such a bright man, always ready to teach what he knew and also to learn something new. I loved his creative mind, his sensitivity and his wonderful sense of humor which brightened each of my days. We were definitely made for each other.

My wonderful wedding with Steve, the Love of my Life

# Chapter 17
## Dad is getting worse

Unfortunately, 3 months after my wedding, I noticed that Dad's writing was changing. We got used to writing faxes back and forth every week. Lately it looked as if his hand was shaking more. The following week, it was even worse. I called to find out that Dad was starting to forget things. He couldn't remember how the VCR was working even though he had been using it every week for the last 20 years. We started worrying about Alzheimer's disease.

Since Dad needed to have inguinal hernia surgery, I decided to fly to Paris to be with him at the time of surgery and to address at the same time the questionable Alzheimer's disease.

As I arrived in Bourg-La-Reine, I noticed that Dad had trouble speaking. It was much worse that I had thought. He needed a head CT scan urgently. Since he was scheduled for hernia surgery the following day, I asked his surgeon to prescribe the head CT scan at his arrival. I was in the radiology room during the scan. As images started to appear on the screen, a huge lesion the size of a peach appeared in his brain. I almost fainted. As I discussed the lesion with the radiologist, we came to the conclusion that there was absolutely no Alzheimer's disease. Instead we had a huge brain tumor, probably a metastasis from his colon cancer. I knew at that Moment that we had lost our battle against cancer. I discretely went to the hospital restroom and cried.

Dad had his hernia surgery as scheduled. I was of course in the operating room with him. He was cold. I made sure he got a blanket covering him to warm him up. I made sure his legs and arms were placed the right way so that we wouldn't have any nerve injury. The surgery went well. After the surgery, the surgeon wanted to keep him a few days in the hospital. Unfortunately the hospital room was very noisy because of construction being done close by. Dad couldn't take the noise. He was so miserable that I had to insist on taking him home. I would do the wound care myself as usual. The surgeon gave his O.K.

When we came back home, I told Mom and Dad about the diagnosis of brain metastasis. Dad knew it was a bad prognosis. I explained to them that it was indeed bad but that I would try as usual to see all the specialists in Paris to find the best possible way to win this battle. In front of them I had a lot of hope. Already 3 years before, everybody had told Dad there was nothing to do for a large liver metastasis but 3 years afterwards, he was still alive and he had a good 3 years. I would find a way. Deep inside of me though, I knew nobody would probably be able to help him this time.

We started Dad on steroids which had a spectacular effect on his brain. He could think normally, talk, write and function normally again. Unfortunately, I knew this would be short lived if we didn't do anything more.

I went to see all the neurosurgeons and all the oncologists in Paris. Nobody wanted to operate. The tumor was too big and above all, it was too deep in the brain. To access it, could prove to be very difficult and very damaging for the structures around. What about chemotherapy? Chemotherapy had worked well so far. The oncologists said that chemotherapy would not go through the blood-brain barrier well. It probably would not be effective on the brain tumor. The only option was radiation therapy but according to everybody it would have a lot of side effects on the brain and would only give him a few more months to live. It wasn't worth it. All the specialists told me to continue steroids as long as they were working. They all told me that with a regular patient, they would try radiations but with a family member, they would not do anything. I knew it was the end.

I went back home and cried again. After I was done crying, I went to see my parents and told them that the only way would be to continue steroids. They understood Dad's condition was terminal with only a short period remaining. Dad was back to his normal self. They decided to travel and enjoy life as long as they could together. Dad said he would call me when the time would be right. I went back to Los Angeles.

Dad had 4 good months. Then little by little, he started getting worse again, having trouble talking and finding words. He could understand everything very well. Only his speech was affected. We had to increase the doses of steroids. This would last 2 weeks then he would get worse again. Soon he started having side effects from steroids with a lot of stomach pain despite anti ulcer medications. Dad couldn't take the pain well. We were on maximum doses of steroids, his stomach pain was increasing despite the meds and he was starting to get worse. His speech was getting worse again and he was starting to have problems walking. He had fallen once already. That's when Dad called me: "Chris, it is time for you to come. Remember, you promised. It is time for me to go." I understood and took the first flight to Paris.

It was August 14th. Here we go again, right in the middle of the summer when every Parisian is on vacation away from Paris. When I arrived at my parents' house, I found Dad in very bad shape. He had lost a lot of weight and had difficulty walking. He was in bed and was having tremendous stomach pain. He was still on a huge dose of steroids and his doctor had started putting him on oral morphine because of the pain. There was nothing more to be done. We were checkmate. I decided to decrease the dose of steroids he was taking. As I did that, his stomach pain decreased. After a week, he didn't have any stomach pain any more. Actually, he didn't have any pain at all in his whole body but his speech started to get worse everyday as well as his walking. On August 20th, as he was getting much worse, we stayed the 3 of us together, listening to Dad's favorite classical music. Mom cooked his favorite meals and we told each other how much we loved each other. On the following day after lunch, Dad said he felt very tired and needed to lie down. We got him comfortable on his bed. Mom and I lay down near him, holding his hand. A few minutes later, he stopped breathing. It was late in the evening on August 21st. The weather was hot and beautiful in Paris. Dad had died peacefully. Mom and I looked at each other and cried in each other's arms.

# Chapter 18
# Dad's funeral

We called Dad's physician who came first thing in the morning on August 22$^{nd}$ to confirm the death and start all the paperwork.

Mom and I went to the mortuary to choose a coffin. Soon afterwards, the mortuary men came to prepare Dad's body. When they placed his body in the coffin, I had to make sure that his head, arms and legs were in a comfortable position. I had done this so many times on operating tables. It had become a habit. I knew he was dead and couldn't feel anything but I still had to do it. We decided to keep his body in our house until the funeral which would be 3 days later.

We put Dad's body in his open coffin in the room next to my bedroom because it was the coolest room in the house. For 3 nights, I slept in the next bedroom. It is a strange feeling to sleep in the room next to your dead Dad. I couldn't sleep well. I was happy when the day of the funeral came. There were very few people at his funeral, only Mom and I and Dad's sister who was 6 years older than him. Our family was very small and Mom hated big crowds. She wanted us to be alone in our grief.

In one way, I was very sad that Dad had passed away. On the other way, I was happy he was gone and had gone peacefully the way he did. I didn't have to worry about him any more. I had worried so much the last 7 years, ever since his colon cancer had been found. I had felt I couldn't rely any more on his physicians' diagnosis or treatments. A lot of those had proved to be costly mistakes. I had decided to get involved at each step of the way and this had been emotionally very heavy for me to carry. Now, I could finally relax and stop worrying. He was good where he was. He looked comfortable. I was happy to accompany him for his last trip to his grave where he would rest peacefully until the end of time.

The funeral went fast. When Mom and I came back home, it seemed empty. We cried again.

Then a whole month of painful paperwork started. Mom was lost and I had to make all the phone calls and prepare all the papers for her to sign. I had to contact insurance companies, social security, his other retirement agencies, the DMV, telephone, gas and water companies. All the bills were in Dad's name. We had to transfer everything to Mom. We had to sell Dad's car. It was a busy September month.

Life is cruel. You work hard your whole life and think you will enjoy your retirement. But when retirement age comes, that's when you get sick. When you are young and can fight diseases easily, you are not sick and you work hard. When you get old and need rest and peace, that's when you get sick and have a lot of pain. Also, when your spouse dies, all you need is peace and quiet to grieve. That's when you have many phone calls to give and a huge amount of paperwork to complete. Those seemed like a mountain to overcome. Fortunately, I was there to help Mom. It still took us one whole month to take care of everything.

Finally after one month, we had time to grieve.

It was extremely difficult for Mom to continue living without Dad. She wanted to die too. I had to convince her that this was only a phase. It would change with time. I called all her friends. I called all her pupils (she was still teaching French on a voluntary basis). I organized her time so that every day she would be busy with something pleasant to do. She slowly got better. When I thought she was out of the woods, I flew back to Los Angeles.

# Chapter 19
# Studying Medicine again

It was a long flight back to LA. I had a lot to think about. So much had happened the last 2 months! I was relieved that Dad had a peaceful passing. It couldn't have been any better for him, or for Mom. I was still worried about Mom but I thought she would make it. I had to concentrate on my life now.

Steve was at the airport to pick me up. I jumped in his arms. I was so happy to be with him again. He looked so good. It felt so wonderful to be in his arms. Although we had been married for almost a year, the following month felt like a honeymoon again. I was happy to be back to life.

I decided to study for the USMLE (United States Medical Licensing Examinations) with my friend Christine. After passing the 3 USMLE, I would be able to apply for a residency in an American hospital. I loved studying. I had studied a major part of my life. It was easy for me. My brain and my body liked being home and studying was allowing me to be home or to study in Westwood with Christine. In between two topics we would go for a walk at the beach or go to the gym. Then we would get back to studying. It was a great schedule and I enjoyed it. It also allowed me to live out my other dream: Acting.

I really loved being on movie sets. One of my secret dreams ever since I was 13 years old was to be an actress. I didn't want to be an actress in France because I wasn't crazy about French acting or French movies.

What I really liked was American acting and American movies. During the months I was studying, I registered at an agency for background work and did extra work on movies. I was thrilled when I got called to be on "The Nutty Professor" with Eddie Murphy. I loved watching main actors rehearse and directors direct them. I loved watching the way make-up people and hair people would come to each lead actor in between takes making sure their skin wasn't too shiny, making sure every single piece of hair was where it should be. I had and still have to this day a tremendous pleasure being on a movie or TV set. On "the Nutty Professor", I got several days of work and this allowed me to be eligible to join the Screen Actors Guild. Shortly after, I proudly joined SAG.

After 6 months of intense studying for each exam, Christine and I finally passed our 3 USMLE exams. We could now apply for a residency - which we did immediately. I had to choose which specialty I wanted. This time around, after many years of practice in France and all over the world with MSF and Club Med, I knew exactly what I wanted to do and what I didn't want to do. There were only 2 specialties I was considering. I wanted to go either into dermatology or into general medicine incorporating Homeopathy and Acupuncture into my practice which is exactly what my Dad had done and exactly what I had been doing for the 7 years I had practiced with him. I started volunteering in dermatology at UC Irvine. Christine started volunteering in psychiatry at USC.

I had heard that it was very hard for a foreign graduate to obtain a residency in the US. Instead of applying for each and every program everywhere in the country which is what most foreign graduates do, I applied for only a few programs, the ones I knew. I especially targeted the hospitals near my house. I didn't want to be far away from Steve for several years. We were still newlyweds and I wanted to come back home to him after work. I knew that my USMLE grades were not good enough to obtain a dermatology residency but it was worth trying.

The day of the residency match came. Christine got the psychiatry residency position she was applying for at USC. I was a little disappointed although not too surprised to see that I didn't match anywhere. In post match, I had an interview at Harbor-UCLA in surgery. They had a position available and they might have residents dropping out in July. A lot of people had warned me against Harbor-UCLA surgical residency program. It had a reputation to be very difficult and physically demanding. Being French, I couldn't believe that any work, especially as a physician could be too difficult. If other people could do it, I could for sure do it too. Harbor-UCLA had the incredible advantage of being 4 miles away from my house.

I didn't get any immediate post match position but in July I got a call from Harbor-UCLA offering me a residency position which I immediately accepted. It was in general surgery but it wasn't a first year position. It was a second year position! As I went there, I had second thoughts. I asked: "Are you sure I can be a safe second year resident in surgery? I am afraid I am not qualified enough. I am only a general practitioner by training. I never had a first year surgical training". The lady in charge of the program reassured me and told me I would be just fine. She even called a 5th year resident to talk to me. He reassured me too telling me that I would never have to operate by myself nor make important decisions by myself. I would always have to refer to a higher authority. He was quite sure I would do just fine. They just had a second year resident quit because the job was too hard for him. They needed me to start right away. I decided to accept the position.

That's when Awe and Hell started for me.

# Chapter 20
# Awe and Hell

"Dr Gilbert, we need you in the operating room. The patient is ready for her breast lumpectomy".

That was my first page on my first day. I felt my heart racing and I started panicking while taking the elevator to go to the operating room. I was not right for the job. I had no idea how to do a breast lumpectomy. I was just a general practitioner. I was not a surgeon by training. I knew a second year surgical position was way above my level. My heart raced even more as I entered the operating room. I started apologizing saying that I didn't have the necessary knowledge nor skill to do that surgery. The nurse reassured me: "The attending will be with you in 10 or 15 minutes. He will help you. You need to get started, get in your sterile gown and drape the patient with sterile drapes. We'll help you."

My heart still racing, I did what she said. I was in scrubs already. I washed my hands, scrubbed them very thoroughly, came in the operating room the way I used to in France 20 years ago. 20 YEARS AGO! That seemed so long ago and that was so far away in my memory! With the help of the scrub nurse, I put on a sterile gown and sterile gloves and started draping the patient. I felt so inadequate. The scrub nurse had to direct all my moves. We were ready to start. The attending was still not there. Finally he arrived, introduced himself, scrubbed in, put on his sterile gown and gloves and joined me. I explained to him my situation and my level of knowledge. He looked not worried at all and said he would help me at each step of the way. He started the surgery himself and when he saw I was getting more comfortable he made me continue and he finished.

There were 4 breast lumpectomies to be done that morning. For the second one, I was already more comfortable. I did the last one almost completely by myself. I had trouble sewing the open wounds back together. The attending was doing beautiful wound closures. This was so important in the breast area. I felt very inadequate again. That day, I put a few surgical needles and threads in my pocket in order to practice at home.

My first afternoon and evening were spent doing rounds on hospitalized patients and admitting new patients.

On my way back at night, I swung by a supermarket to buy a large quantity of chicken wings. When I got back home, Steve took me in his arms saying: "How was your first day as a surgeon?" Without answering anything, I smiled and put all the chicken wings on the kitchen counter under Steve's puzzled look. I cut open the first one, got a surgical needle and thread out and started repairing the wound, explaining to Steve what had happened that day. Steve started laughing. I laughed too. We just couldn't stop. Still laughing, I handed him a knife and I asked him to make several wounds on 2 extra chicken wings. I was going to repair them. He did as I asked him to do. My wound repairs were really bad. I would have to practice a lot to improve my style.

From then on, every evening, coming back from the hospital, Steve had more and more difficult open chicken skin wounds for me to repair. Every evening he would smile watching me try to repair the wounds. I got better fast and after a few days, I was able to repair wounds beautifully like my attending surgeon. This rotation was called GI onc. Rotation which stands for Gastro Intestinal and Oncology rotation. That turned out to be an "easy" rotation.

The following rotation, Awe and Hell started. It was a cardiothoracic surgery rotation. Awe because of the awesome cases we had and the awesome training I got. Hell because of the horrible work hours and call schedule.

We were doing a lot of CABG which are Coronary Artery Bypass Graft surgeries for people having blockages in their coronary arteries. In the operating room, I was in charge of harvesting the saphenous vein during the time the attending was opening the patient's thorax to get to his or her heart. It was a fantastic and spectacular surgery each time. Occasionally I was helping the thoracic part of the surgery. I was in Awe when holding the patient's beating heart in my hand. I was in Awe watching the attending locate all the blockages in all the coronary arteries and bypassing them with bits and pieces of the saphenous vein I was providing. Harvesting the vein was hard for me to learn. I had to locate the vein and open the patient's leg in its entire length taking care of the bleeding along the way. Then I had to get the vein out which was not as simple as it sounds because it had a lot of small ramifications that would bleed very easily. Then I had to close the whole length of the wound layer by layer. I had to do this fairly quickly because the attending was waiting for that precious vein. I was not too good at the beginning. I got better at the end of the rotation.

Hell was the call schedule and work hours. I had to start pre-rounds on my patients at 5:30 am everyday. We were starting rounds at the patients' bedside at 6:30 am. Then at 7:30 am we needed to be in the operating room. We operated the whole day then, I had to do pre-rounds again, take care of newly admitted patients and discharge others. Then we did evening rounds. I was lucky if I was getting home before 8:00 pm. Then I had to start pre-rounds the following day again at 5:30 am. In addition to this, I had to be on call at night every 3rd night. This included taking care of patients that just had surgery in the cardiac ICU. I was allowed to have one day off per week but in reality most interns and residents only had one day off per month. That was Hell. The nights on call were usually busy and I was usually paged every 15 to 30 minutes. I was lucky if I could sleep 45 minutes of uninterrupted sleep.

One day, we admitted a patient who just had a gun shot wound to the chest. The patient was bleeding heavily in the emergency room. My attending and I had no time to transfer the patient to the operating room. We had to crack his chest open right there in the ER. My attending got his hand behind the heart while I tried to suction all the blood rapidly shooting everywhere. He found a hole in the aorta and managed to place his finger against it. That minimized the bleeding and gave us time to transfer the patient to the OR. I had to take over with my finger against the aorta hole during the transfer. We managed to save the patient. That was amazing.

Another spectacular event was when I got called by the OB department. A woman had just delivered her baby 3 days prior and now was suddenly getting short of breath. She was probably having a pulmonary artery embolism and could die shortly. Her blood pressure was starting to drop. I called my attending who told me to transfer her to the operating room urgently. As I did so, her heart stopped. She was in full cardiac arrest when she entered the OR. We had to start external cardiac compressions for a few minutes then crack her sternum open. My attending placed my hand around her heart and told me to do a cardiac massage. I had never done this. He showed me how to do it. It was very emotional for me. Here I was, holding and pumping the heart of a young mother. Her heart seemed small yet very muscular. I was keeping her alive with my hand! During that time, my attending put her on bypass then opened the pulmonary artery. He found a large blood clot there and removed it. It was a large pulmonary embolism. Those are usually deadly. After removing the clot, we tried to get her off bypass and have her heart work by itself again. Unfortunately, it wouldn't. We applied progressively more potent electric shocks directly to the heart. It would start for a few minutes then stop again. We used drugs, electric shocks and cardiac massages for one hour trying to revive her. We couldn't. She died. When I looked up, I was surprised to see a lot of interns, residents and attendings in the room. The whole hospital had heard about that spectacular case and the people were taking turns to be in the room and watch us.

I did indeed learn a lot during that rotation. I learned how to place central venous catheters, arterial lines and pleural tubes. I learned how to do cardiac bypass surgeries and place new heart valves.

My next rotation was Neurosurgery. I was in Awe when the attending surgeon taught me how to open a human skull to get to the brain. I was in Awe touching my first human brain. I learned that a brain is highly vascularized and can bleed a lot. If a brain starts bleeding, sometimes it is impossible to stop it.

We had a 20 year old young man brought in by paramedics one day after a motorcycle accident. I had a head CT scan done on him and saw that his brain was bleeding. We had to operate to stop the bleeding. I opened the skull with an electric saw. When I got to the brain, I saw that a lot of small vessels were bleeding diffusely. My attending tried to stop the bleeding. It was hard to do. There were too many small vessels bleeding. When we finally managed to stop the bleeding, we put the patient's skull back on his brain and sent the patient back to the ICU. The following CT scan showed that he had started bleeding again, this time more heavily than the first time. We brought him back to the OR and opened his skull again. We tried to stop the bleeding, did as much as we could then closed. One day later, a new head CT showed an even more intense bleeding. We brought him back to the OR for the 3rd time but couldn't stop the bleeding. At that time hundreds of small vessels in his brain were bleeding. We cauterized as many as we could and closed for the last time. Unfortunately the patient continued bleeding heavily. The following day he died. This made me understand why wearing a helmet is so important when being on a motorcycle or for any dangerous sport.

Another case stayed in my mind. I was called one day by the ER to examine a 35 year old woman. She was strikingly beautiful. She was in great physical shape doing body building everyday. She was accompanied by her fiancé. They were planning on getting married the following month. She was complaining of weakness in her left hand and arm. This had started one week prior, had gotten slightly better for a few days and was now getting worse. I examined her and found no other significant element than a very slight muscular weakness in her left hand. I sent her for a brain MRI and to my surprise saw a mass in her right brain about 3 centimeters diameter. I discussed the mass with the radiologist who pointed out to me one smaller mass about 1.5

centimeters diameter in another area of her brain. Together, we started looking closely at the whole MRI and found 9 other masses ranging from 0.5 to 1cm diameter. She had a total of 11 brain tumors. I was in shock. According to the radiologist, the most likely diagnosis with such an MRI on a young woman was brain metastasis of cutaneous melanoma. I went back to my patient and asked her about her previous sun exposures. She said she used to lie down in the sun for hours in order to get a nice tan. She was still doing it from time to time but not as much as she used to. I told her what the MRI had shown. She started crying.

Shortly after, we scheduled her for a brain tumor biopsy which showed metastatic melanoma. I looked at her skin but couldn't find any lesion on her skin at all. I learned that skin cancers triggered by sun exposure can appear and disappear spontaneously. When they disappear, they can metastasize. Their favorite spot to metastasize to is the brain.

With 11 tumors in her brain, the prognosis was poor. We offered her to start chemotherapy and radiation therapy explaining to her that it was probably only palliative and would not cure her. We didn't know any treatment to cure her. She decided not to do anything. Later I learned that she got married as scheduled and went on a wonderful honeymoon. She died 6 months later.

That taught me another lesson. It taught me how dangerous prolonged sun exposure can be. From that day on, I have been using 30 to 50 index protection sunscreen everyday on my skin and wearing a hat, long sleeve shirt and pants when walking outside in the sun.

A few weeks later, it was time to start my next rotation. It was an ICU rotation. I was scared already. I didn't know if I could handle the call schedule. On that particular rotation, I had to be on call every other night for one month. I had to start pre-rounds at 5:30 am to be ready for rounds with the attending at 6:30 am. I then had to work the whole day, be on call the whole night, work the following day until 4:00 pm and sometimes 6:00 pm then go back home, rest, sleep one night then start again with pre-rounds at 5:30 am and so on for the whole month. As for nights on call, I would be lucky if I slept 15 minutes of uninterrupted sleep. This basically meant that I had to work a minimum of 34 hours non-stop then be off work and sleep for 12 hours then start again with 34 hours of work. This didn't seem humanly possible for me to do. I wasn't sure my body could take this kind of abuse. I was puzzled. I couldn't understand. This was a hospital. We were physicians. My attendings were all physicians and they were letting this kind of physical abuse happen? Didn't they know that such a schedule was grossly unhealthy? Well obviously they didn't!

That's when pure HELL started.

# Chapter 21
# Pure Hell

Dring! Dring! Dring! That was my alarm clock! I looked at the time. It was 5:00 am. I had to get up. I had learned how to get up and get ready to go in 10 minutes. I put on my scrubs quickly, said good morning and good bye to my husband still asleep. At 5:14 am I was out of the door. At 5:30 am I was pre-rounding on my ICU patients. At 6:30 am I was doing rounds with the attending. At 7:30 am I had a list of procedures to do including changing IV central lines in quite a few patients but it would be done later after the 7:30 am Morbidity and Mortality conference and the 8:30 am Grand Rounds conference. I also had to prepare a lecture the attending had asked me to give the following week. I might have a few minutes to do it later that day in between 2 admissions. I was on call that day. I was starting to be really exhausted after one week of calls every other day. The calls were really tiring and I was getting paged every 5 minutes either by the ER for a new admission or by the ICU for a problem with a patient. I started feeling feverish with aches and pains everywhere. It felt like I was getting sick. I knew this call schedule was really unhealthy for me. I was pushing my body too much. I was completely sleep deprived and needed rest!

A nurse called me: "Dr. Gilbert, your patient's blood pressure is dropping". That was a patient admitted a few hours prior for gun shot wounds to his right leg and arm. I went to his bedside and examined him. His abdomen was very painful. He was probably having internal abdominal bleeding. I called my attending who told me to prepare him for a peritoneal test. A few minutes later, he was with me and we were inserting a needle in the patient's abdomen. We found blood in his peritoneal cavity. We had to take him urgently to the OR. I scrubbed in. When we opened his abdomen, blood started shooting out. The patient's spleen was injured and his whole abdomen was filled with blood. We had to resect his spleen and give him a blood transfusion. The surgery was successful and very spectacular. Two hours later the patient was back in the ICU.

It was time for me to have a quick lunch in the cafeteria. I still had 4 central lines to change and 2 abdominal lavages to do. My pager rang. It was the ER. "Dr. Gilbert, we have a new admission for you. You need to come immediately". I said I was on my way. Two seconds later, my pager rang again. This time it was the ICU: "Dr. Gilbert, your patient Mr. Gross is having trouble breathing. You need to come immediately." Ten seconds later, I got another page. It was the ER again for another admission. I felt my heart pounding. I would never have time to do every thing I needed to do that day. I probably wouldn't have time to get my precious 15 minutes of sleep that night. It was the beginning of a busy day. I started feeling sicker. My throat was aching and I started coughing.

I went to the patient getting short of breath first. He had fluid in his pleural cavity. I had to put a tube in his chest. Then I went to the ER to admit an acute pancreatitis patient and a patient with possible appendicitis.

It was 5 pm when I started with my procedures of the day. There were 2 patients in the ICU with necrotizing pancreatitis. They had been operated on the previous week but their bowel had been too dilated to close their abdomen. They had been left with their abdomen open and only a sterile piece of plastic covering it. Everyday, a resident had to open the plastic cover, sterily dress the field and wash the internal organs in the abdomen with sterile saline while still at the bedside. This was the duty of the person on call. That day it was me. I had to remove all necrotized tissue at the bedside. The colon and small intestine were very dilated and it took me forever to wash everything. Then, I had to sew the plastic cover back to the patients' skin to cover their abdomen. Everyday, the plastic had to be sewn back to the skin which was extremely painful for the patients. Since we couldn't do a general anesthesia everyday, we were giving them a small quantity of morphine but they still felt the pain. It seemed to me very cruel to do this procedure everyday. But I wasn't there to give my opinion. I was in training and I had to follow orders. I did the 2 abdominal washings.

I was about to start changing the first of 4 central lines when I got paged again. It was 8:00 pm. It was the ER. "Dr. Gilbert, we have another admission for you. It is a MVA." MVA stands for Motor Vehicle Accident. I asked what the patient had. The nurse said he had broken ribs and a pneumothorax. The emergency room resident had just placed a chest tube. The patient was in stable condition which meant that I had time to swing by the cafeteria to have a quick bite to eat for dinner. I was feeling more and more feverish and I was starting to get a very productive continuous cough. I was getting worse by the minute. I went by the pharmacy to take 2 Tylenol.

It was 10:00 pm when I left the ER to come back to the ICU to attempt again to change the first of 4 central lines. I got paged many times in between but I finally managed to change the 4 lines. I looked at the time. It was 2 am. At 5:30 am, I needed to pre-round on my patients to be ready for the 6:30 am rounds. I was exhausted. I was coughing every 5 minutes. I needed sleep. I decided to go to my on-call room.

The on-call room was a very tiny room big enough to fit 4 bunk beds. There was no window. Three other residents were using the other 3 beds. I took the 4th bed and lied down. One second later, I heard a pager. Fortunately, it wasn't mine. It was the pager of the resident on the bed above mine. He got up to answer his page. Soon after, I heard another pager ring. This time, it was mine. I looked at the time. I only had 3 minutes to lie down. That wasn't much. I answered my page. It was the ER again. I had another admission. This time it was an old lady with abdominal pain. I went down and diagnosed an acute cholecystitis. During the time I was in the ER, I got paged by the ICU. A patient was having a rapid heart rate. Another patient was in pain. I addressed the problems.

It was 5:15 am when I got back to my on-call bed. I was coughing non-stop at that time and was taking Tylenol every 4 hours. I was feeling horrible. I had to get up at 5:30 am which means that if I was lucky I could have 15 minutes of sleep. 15 minutes of sleep… that sounded so good. I prayed to God to be able to get those precious 15 minutes without my pager interrupting them.

Fifteen minutes later, my alarm clock rang. I looked at the clock. It was 5:30 am. I felt grateful. I did manage to get 15 minutes of sleep this night. This was awesome. Suddenly I felt my chest hurting and a very deep productive cough came out of my lungs. I remembered I was sick. I had to swing by the pharmacy to get antibiotics. I had to hurry because I had to pre-round on my patients.

At 6:30 am, I already had my first dose of antibiotics and I was ready to round on my patients with the attending. I knew I looked horrible. I was coughing non-stop. I was feeling sicker and sicker by the minute despite anti-inflammatory drugs and antibiotics which I had just started. During the whole 2 hours of rounds, while I was presenting all the new admissions of the night to the attending I coughed. It was a very loud and productive cough. I had a high fever. Do you think that in 2 hours of rounds the attending commented on my cough? If you think so, well you are wrong. Nobody, I repeat, nobody commented on my cough. None of the 10 people around me said: "Dr. Gilbert, you sound so sick, you need to go back home and get some rest". Instead, I heard "Dr. Gilbert, now that you have done the admissions, you need to do procedures on each of your patients. Also, don't forget, you have a presentation to prepare for. Your presentation is in 2 days." My presentation! I had forgotten all about it. I needed to go to the library. When would I have time to do it? I only had this evening and night to sleep then I had to get up at 5:30 am to be on call again then the following morning I had to present! This was completely inhumane! This was completely unhealthy! And guess what? The people who were creating this absurd unhealthy schedule were physicians!!!!

My colleague didn't tell me: "Chris, you look very sick. Go home and I'll take over your tasks". He was under as much pressure as me and he was alternating calls with me. I looked around and realized there was nobody else to take over my work. I had to get healthy quickly.

I tried looking at the situation with a humoristic point of view. After all, it was quite funny. Here I was in an ICU, coughing my brains out in front of very weak and easily prone to infections patients who actually seemed healthier than me. I knew I was very contagious. I could have infected the entire ICU. That's how much I was coughing. Legally I really needed to go home, first because legally I was allowed to be a human being and sleep and second because, I was probably an infectious danger for all the weak ICU patients. This made me feel stronger.

Unfortunately, I realized it was the week-end. It was Sunday morning. Days of the week didn't matter any more on that particular rotation. Every other day on call was every other day on call no matter if it was a week day or a week-end. In fact week-ends were busier than week days. I realized I just finished a Saturday night call. That's why the ER was so busy. We were Sunday morning! That's why the attending was taking all the time in the world to comment on each case. He probably had a good night sleep and had nothing else to do that day. We had started rounds 2 hours prior and he was still explaining among other things the differences between hypovolemic and septic shock. He had to talk in a loud voice to cover my very loud constant coughing. I wanted him to stop. I still had procedures to do and I really needed to get some rest. It was noon when he finally stopped. I got a quick bite to eat. I was about to collapse. After lunch, I got my procedures done, probably infected the whole ICU and finally drove back home.

Yes, I drove back home. I was lucky I was only 4 miles away from my house because I was falling asleep at each red light. Now I could understand why one month ago, a resident from another hospital had a car accident while driving back after a call night and died. It was on the news. Our call schedule was so unhealthy that it was putting our lives at risk. I was indeed a dangerous driver too.

It was 5:00 pm when I arrived home. I had 12 hours to rest and get back in shape. I had to be back at the hospital at 5:30 am the following morning to be on call again. I couldn't think any more. I took a quick shower and fell on my bed. One second later I was fast asleep.

My night was very agitated. I woke up very often to cough. My cough was getting worse despite the antibiotics.

At 5:00 am, when the alarm clock rang, I felt a heavy weight on my chest. A few seconds later a very violent cough shook my whole body. A large amount of green sputum came out of my lungs into my mouth. I spit it out. I felt feverish. I checked my temperature. It was 101. I had to get dressed quickly. I was on call again today. I took 2 Tylenol and another dose of antibiotics, kissed my husband good morning and good bye and drove to the hospital.

I was in very bad shape when I did my pre-rounds and then rounds with the attending. It was obvious that I was really sick. My cough was constant and very loud. At the end of rounds. instead of getting the wished for "Dr. Gilbert, you seem very sick, go back home and rest" I got "Dr. Gilbert, during your call today you will need to change 5 lines and do 3 abdominal washings". I didn't think I could survive 34 hours of non-stop work again. Not only that but I had to prepare for my presentation the following day. My heart started racing. That's when it started to skip beats. I could feel for the first time in my life my heart beating very strongly and fast, then suddenly it would stop, skip one or 2 beats then start again faster for 3 beats then back to normal. Then a few seconds later, it would skip beats again. I got very worried. Was I going to kill myself for this residency? Was it worth it? I asked myself. My answer was no. I had to take care of myself. Obviously nobody else would. I was in no shape to be on call. I was in no shape to work in an ICU. I had to get some rest.

I went to the attending. I told him that I was feeling too sick to be on call, that I had a fever, a productive cough despite being on antibiotics and that I was starting to have an irregular heart beat. I told him I would not be able to do my presentation the following day. I needed to go home. To my surprise, he seemed very unhappy. He told me that I couldn't go just yet. First, I had to find somebody to cover the ICU and ER call for me today. As for the presentation, he was sorry I couldn't present because he was counting on me. I would present the following week instead. I thanked him and left.

It took me one hour to find a resident willing to take my call. I had to find somebody from another rotation. A friend of mine in the GI Oncology rotation accepted to take over. I was relieved. I quickly drove back home. At noon that day, I was in bed again. It was my first sick day in 10 years. I stayed in bed for 3 days. It was heavenly.

For the first time in my life, I was appreciating being able to sleep without any pager or alarm clock waking me up. Silence was heavenly! Being naked in freshly washed sheets was heavenly.

I remembered my time in Sri Lanka when after 3 months of no bath or hot water I learned how to appreciate hot baths. Until this day I am enjoying hot showers and hot baths to no end.

This time, I learned that having a quiet night of uninterrupted sleep was very precious. I decided that never again in my entire life would I complain about not being able to sleep at night. Never in my entire life would I take sleeping pills. I would always remember this time when 15 minutes of uninterrupted sleep per night was a luxury. I would always remember this intense heavenly feeling of the simple pleasure of getting naked into freshly washed sheets with silence surrounding me. This was enough for my happiness!

After 3 days in bed, I felt much better. I was coughing much less and my heart was back with a regular rhythm. At 5:30 am the following day, I was back at work. I managed to finish this month of every other night on call but it was physically very hard. I knew it was illegal to ask us, residents to have such a schedule but everybody else was doing it without complaining. I was one of the only foreign graduates of the program. Everybody was American and nobody was complaining. I didn't want to be the only one to complain and give a bad opinion of the French people. I decided to keep my mouth shut.

The rest of the year went by very quickly. Every month, I was starting a new rotation. I learned a lot. It was a tremendous experience. I learned how to do laparoscopic cholecystectomies by myself. I learned how to remove spleens, how to operate on pancreas, colons, breasts, hearts, lungs. I was in awe most of the days despite the very physically hard and demanding schedule.

During that year, I continued to apply for a Dermatology residency position but I didn't get any. My grades were too low and the positions were only given to the best American medical students in the country. I decided to give up on Dermatology.

I decided to be a General Practitioner adding Homeopathy and Acupuncture to my practice just like what I used to do in France. In order to be a General Practitioner, I had to have a valid medical license in California. Unfortunately, a new law had just passed stating that instead of needing only one year of practical medical training in an American accredited program, medical students now needed 2 years. I almost fainted when I heard that. That meant I had to do another year of training.

My last week of my surgical residency year was lighter. I was only on call once that week. It was an easier rotation. The attending offered me to stay one more year. This way at the end of that extra year I would be able to get my California medical license. I thanked him but I refused. I knew that one extra year like this could kill me. It was physically too hard for me and I was not getting any younger. Although I didn't have any regrets about this year, I had to find an easier program for my second year. Most of my friends in the Surgery Residency program would have the same physically challenging schedule for 6 years. I felt sorry for them.

My last day was wonderful. I could appreciate Harbor-UCLA again. I took the time to eat lunch that day. At 7 pm, I said goodbye to my friends and drove home, singing in my car.

I had been home for a good 3 weeks and I was getting used to it. It took some time to get to know my husband again and get back in shape. We started walking again. The first week, I couldn't walk fast. I was getting short of breath after just a few steps. The second week was better and by the 3rd week, I was my usual self again, walking, going to the gym and enjoying life tremendously. It was time to look for another year of medical training in an accredited program. I called all the programs. We were in August and maybe somebody had dropped out somewhere. The answers were negative everywhere. No position was available.

I decided to go back to UC Irvine to volunteer in Dermatology again. On my way to the Dermatology department, I decided to stop by the Internal Medicine department at the Long Beach VA. The head of the program was in his office. I asked to talk to him to let him know that I was interested in an internship year or a residency year. To my surprise he said: "Dr. Gilbert, I am happy to meet you. As a matter of fact, this is a good timing, one of our interns just dropped out of the program this morning. Would you be interested in taking over his position starting tomorrow?" My heart started pounding. That was indeed a very lucky timing. A year in Internal Medicine would be a piece of cake compared to the 2nd year in Surgery I just had. I accepted right away.

The following day, I started my second year of training which was in fact a first year of internship in Internal Medicine. The entire year took place at the Long Beach Veteran Administration Hospital. That year was so much easier than the previous year. I was on call every 4th night only. On some call nights, I could sleep one or 2 hours, sometimes more. It was great although I learned much less than in Surgery. I discovered I was excellent at making surgical diagnosis. One day, I was called by the ER to examine an obese patient with a painful abdomen. I diagnosed a possible acute pancreatitis, wanted to admit the patient and schedule him for an urgent abdominal CT scan. My second year resident refused and told me not to admit the patient. For him, since all the blood tests were normal, the patient needed to go back home and just eat less to lose weight. I fought him and we had to call the attending physician. The attending came, took the second year resident's side but having second thoughts, he looked at me and said: "Dr. Gilbert, what would you do to prove your diagnosis?"

Me: "I would like to admit the patient for at least one day. He needs to be NPO (nothing per mouth). I'll manage to get an urgent abdominal CT scan and that will probably show a pancreatitis."

The attending: "O.K. I'll give you 24 hours to prove your diagnosis."

I thanked him. The following day, it took me half an hour to convince the radiologist to do an urgent abdomen CT scan for my new patient. The schedule was completely booked and there was only one spot kept for an emergency. For him, my patient didn't qualify as an emergency. After much work, I finally managed to convince him to do the CT scan the same day. I was curious to see what the result was. I had never fought a higher hierarchy before. My year of surgery although incredibly painful had given me an extra sense. When I was placing my hands on an abdomen, I could immediately tell when it was a surgical abdomen or not. I knew this patient's abdomen was surgical. My hands could tell. I wasn't surprised when the CT scan showed a very severe acute pancreatitis.

Both the attending and my second year resident were very surprised at my correct diagnosis. The patient indeed had an acute pancreatitis. As a consequence, his entire bowel was paralyzed. The patient had to be admitted for one week. He had to be placed on IV nutrition and nothing by mouth to decrease the inflammation. From that day on, I had the respect of everyone in the program.

The rest of the year went by fast. The night calls were easy. I often had 2 to 3 hours of sleep per call. It was still very painful to hear my pager in the middle of the night but it was nothing compared to the year before. The major improvement is that I had one full day off per week and that was so wonderful. At the VA, residents and interns were respected as human beings and that felt so good.

At the end of the year, UCI offered me to stay in the program to complete 2 more years of Internal Medicine residency. I declined. I now qualified to apply for a California medical license. I could open my private practice as a General Practitioner in California. I had enough of night calls. I needed rest. I said goodbye to everybody and I drove back home singing in my car.

# Chapter 22
# Living my Dream

All my paperwork was sent to Sacramento and I was waiting to obtain my California Medical License. This could take a few months which meant that I had a few months to enjoy life and try living my dream.

My dream was to be on movie sets in front of a camera. Since I was a SAG member (Screen Actors Guild), I attended the acting class of the SAG conservatory and loved it. When I was acting, I was feeling high. This is a feeling that is difficult to explain. I felt and I am still nowadays feeling like I am flying above clouds when I perform. Nothing else exists. I start getting in the character's mind and suddenly I take off. My whole body changes and I become the character. I react to other characters with a wide range of emotions going from anger to sadness to happiness. Being able to express all those emotions and more in front of an audience and in front of a camera is incredible. The audience loves it and I do too. When my part is over, it leaves me in awe. This feeling fulfills me completely. It seems that I need nothing more in my life.

Soon I heard about a TV series being shot in LA. It was called "Strong Medicine". I contacted the person in charge of hiring the background people working on the show. Soon afterwards, I got a call from Entertainment Partners asking me if I could be on the set within the hour. They needed somebody that could act as a practical nurse at a patient's bedside immediately. My heart started racing. This was the Dream of my Life! I could be on a Hollywood set! I was ecstatic! I said yes and within 20 minutes was on the set of "Strong Medicine".

As I arrived in the parking lot, a guard stopped me: "Sorry, you cannot enter, this is crew parking for a TV show". I proudly said "Yes, I know, I am part of the TV show, my name is Chris Gilbert and I was just called to be a practical nurse. It is a rush call." The guard looked at his list, found my name and with a big smile welcomed me in the parking lot. It was wonderful! Here I was entering my dream place. I quickly parked. As I got out of my car, I saw a lot of activity outside. They were shooting an outdoor scene. I could see the main actors, director, assistant directors, make-up people, light people and grips. I stayed there a few minutes wondering if I was dreaming. This was heaven for me. A beautiful lady with a walkie-talkie came to me and introduced herself as the 2nd Assistant Director: "Chris, we need you for the next scene, go to wardrobe and get some scrubs, then go to props where they will give you a name badge and a stethoscope. When you'll be all set, come to me. Hurry, we'll need you in a few minutes."

As if in a dream, walking on clouds, I went to wardrobe then to props. Everybody was so nice to me. I put on burgundy scrubs. I needed a stethoscope, a penlight, a pen and a name badge which the props people gave me. Soon I was all set. A few minutes later, I was looking for the 2nd AD again. She came rushing to me: "We are moving to the next scene. It takes place in the emergency room. We need you to help the main actor with a cardiac arrest."

As I entered the emergency room, Suzie the medical advisor came to me to introduce herself and explain to me what I was expected to do. One patient was being brought to the ER in cardiac arrest. I was supposed to ride on the gurney with her while doing chest compressions then help transfer her to the ER bed then the lead actors Rosa Blasi and Brennan Elliott would take over. I got introduced to Rosa and Brennan who were really nice to me. We did the scene several times. Each time, I had a blast. It was a high pace scene which was perfect for me. I was so happy. I was living my Dream.

This started a long relationship with the show that lasted 2 years. For the following 2 years, I was called fairly often to be either in the operating room, emergency room or at a patient's bedside. I played the part of either a surgeon or a practical nurse. In the operating room, the crew liked to have me play with all the surgical instruments. I was great at using pick-ups and needle holders, making believe that I was sawing a layer of tissue or muscle. The director loved it when I was making believe the patient was heavily bleeding. I was pretending using suction, dipping white laparotomy sponges in the open surgical field and pulling them out filled with fake blood, making believe I was looking for the bleeder and cauterizing it. I started knowing Jeanine Turner then Patricia Richardson the following year. I tried getting a speaking part on the show but unfortunately I never got any. They probably didn't like my French accent. It didn't matter. I was happy being on the set and working with the lead actors.

Later that year, I got called on the TV show "ER" where I played an anesthesiologist then on "The Agency" where I was featured as nurse Maya Gallin. It was a 2 day shoot. There too I had a non speaking role but it was an important one. I was the only background actress for 3 days on the set so, I was with the lead actors all the time. I had a lot of coverage with great close-ups. My character got shot at the end of the episode. I had a great time pretending getting shot, falling on the ground and playing dead with my eyes open. It was wonderful. I could feel the camera turning above my head, focusing on me. I was careful not to move my eyes and not to breathe too deeply so that my chest wouldn't move. I loved it.

Shortly after, I got my first speaking part on the TV show: "Family Law". First I was hired as a background person. They needed someone to play a doctor in an emergency room. When I arrived, they upgraded me to a speaking emergency room physician. The director wanted more activity in the ER. He wanted me to give orders to the nurses who had to hurry and do what I was asking. I had to sign my first contract as an paid actress. I was in heaven!

I also started doing medical advising on sets. I was called on the TV show JAG and later on NCIS then on several commercials to be a medical adviser. Most of the time, I was in charge of preparing an ER scene. I had to hook background actors to IVs and heart monitors, then, when the main actor would arrive, I was in charge of his dressings, oxygen mask and heart monitor. I was working more closely with the director and this was wonderful. Being a medical adviser was great but it was a lot of work and long hours. The pay was much better than background acting but I missed being in front of the camera. I loved working with the different property managers, directors and producers. It was a great experience.

In the meantime, I had received my California Medical License and thus was ready to start opening my private medical practice. I postponed it as much as I could, enjoying being part of the Hollywood world. I postponed it for 2 years, trying to get more speaking parts. Unfortunately, my French accent was probably too strong and since I wasn't getting any younger, I didn't get any more speaking parts. It was time to look for a medical office and open my private practice.

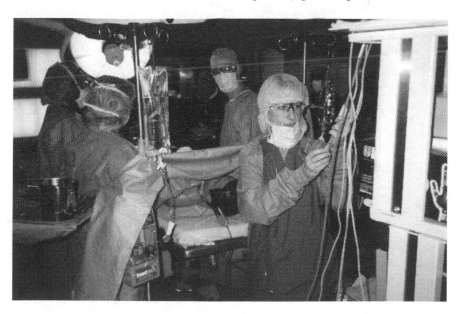

On the set of the TV show "ER" (I played an anesthesiologist)

# Chapter 23
## Opening my private medical practice

I didn't want to work far away from home, so I looked for an office in Torrance. I wanted to recreate the kind of practice I had in France. This would take some work.

It took me one month to explore all the medical office buildings near my house. I didn't like any of them. I didn't feel good in any of them. They were either too big, too small, they had not enough windows or they were too cold.

I wanted to see patients only 2 days per week and work long hours during those 2 days. All I needed was to find another physician with the kind of office I liked who would be ready to share her or his office space for those 2 days. Again, I started exploring all the office spaces to share in Torrance. There were only 4. I didn't like any of those 4. I then decided to visit all the different physicians in the area to introduce myself and if I liked their office, to ask if they would be willing to have me use it 2 days a week. That took 4 months. I was in no hurry. I knew exactly what I wanted. I wanted an office that had large windows with a lot of sunlight, oriented anywhere but north. I wanted an office that had very little air conditioning. I couldn't stand air conditioning because I was always too cold. Even when I was working in Africa, I couldn't stand air conditioning. I had no trouble taking the heat but my body was miserable in the cold. I wanted a very cozy and warm office with nice personal decorations preferably on a high floor with a nice view.

After 4 months, I hadn't found anything I liked. That's when my husband pointed out to me a small office building on Torrance Blvd which only had 5 floors. As I entered it the following day, I noticed that all the physicians there were owners. I went straight to the highest 5th floor and knocked on one door. As I entered the waiting room, my mouth remained open in awe. The decoration was awesome, very warm and personal with water fountains, wind charms, flowers and green plants everywhere. I immediately felt incredibly good there. I glanced at the office itself. It was very tiny but with huge windows, oriented south. I could see a lot of sunlight coming from those windows. The air conditioned was very mild. I immediately fell in love with the place.

I introduced myself to the receptionist Darlene and said I was looking for an office space to share. All I needed were 2 days a week. She told me to wait. She was going to talk to Dr. Joselyn Bailey, the owner. I was thinking that there were probably very few chances that the owner would say yes but it was worth trying. The longer I was staying in this office, the more comfortable I felt.

A very beautiful lady came out of her office. She was Dr. Bailey, specialist in Nephrology and Internal Medicine. I complimented her for her office decorations. I immediately loved her. She asked me about myself and my resume and to my surprise, immediately said that she would consider sharing her office space with me. I had tears coming to my eyes. I shook her hand and thanked her. That was it. I had found the office I would work in for many years.

We did some paper work and I opened my practice at the beginning of December 2002.

I started practicing only General Medicine but quickly I realized that most of my patients would benefit from Homeopathy and Acupuncture which is what I had been doing in France. That's when I decided to recreate exactly the kind of practice I had in France. My practice became: General Medicine, Homeopathy and Acupuncture. I thought I would be one of many physicians having this kind of practice in LA. I had the shock of my life. Very few physicians had a similar practice.

Most physicians in LA were spending 5 to 15 minutes with each patient, going after the money rather than the quality of work. I couldn't work like this. They were getting burnt out and depressed but still continued that kind of practice. I knew that kind of practice. That's how Harbor UCLA and the Long Beach VA had trained me. I hated that. I decided to go against the national rule and habit. I decided to create my own way of working and spend at least one hour with each patient. Each of them would be special and my focus would be on their well being rather than on the money.

Very quickly, I started having more and more patients. My way of working was so different than other physicians that my existing patients would tell their family and friends about me. Soon after, I got their whole family and friends as patients.

By spending one hour with each patient, I had time to review their past medical history and all their medications. I had time to ask about the origin and trigger of each of their symptoms. I discovered that a lot of patients were taking too many medications. Each time they would go to their doctor for a different complaint, another medication would be added. Nobody had taken the time to see if they really needed such strong medications or if after 6 months, the medications were still needed. Most physicians were looking for a quick fix and not looking at the whole picture.

I was asking each patient to bring all the dietary supplements they were taking and I noticed that many of them were taking too many supplements. Some supplements interacted with their regular medications. None of their regular physicians had asked about dietary supplements.

I found that many patients reacted well to Homeopathy and Acupuncture. Very often with only a homeopathic treatment and one acupuncture session, I would be able to avoid giving a conventional medication. Only if the symptom persisted would I give a regular medication. One day, Mrs. O, a young and beautiful 28 year old brunette lady came to see me for headaches. She had those headaches almost every day for the last 3 years. They were located at the back of her head and were triggered by strong emotions and bad news. She was also complaining of emotional diarrhea. She had seen several physicians but couldn't stand the side effects of the various conventional medications they had given her. I gave her the homeopathic medication Gelsemium Sempervirens 12 C, 5 pellets under the tongue 3 times a day. I also did an acupuncture session on her. Within one week, she got better and within one month she was almost headache free.

Gelsemium 12 C is made with Yellow Jasmine diluted 12 times 100 times. The more diluted it is, the more potent it is. Since she got much better on Gelsemium 12 C, 3 months later, I gave her Gelsemium 30 C which is Yellow Jasmine diluted 30 times 100 times. Now, she only has mild headaches once or twice a year. The big advantage of homeopathy is that there is no known side effect or drug interaction because the medications are extremely diluted.

Later, Mrs. O referred her mother to me. Mrs. W was 55 years old, suffering from depression. Her depression had started at menopause. She had a lot of hot flashes and didn't want to have sex with her husband any more. All she wanted was to be left alone. She didn't want to be touched or talked to. She didn't want any antidepressant because of the possible side effects. I started her on Sepia 12 C, 5 pellets under the tongue 3 times a day and also did an acupuncture session on her. Sepia 12 C is made with Cuttlefish ink diluted 12 times one hundred times. One week later, she was much better and one month later, she was transformed. She had started dance classes and was feeling much happier. Again, we had no side effects or drug interactions.

The theory behind homeopathy is that "like cures like": A very diluted dose of a particular plant, mineral or animal extract treats symptoms that could be generated by the same extract if given in toxic doses. For example a large dose of onion will give us runny nose and watery eyes. When a patient comes to me complaining of a cold with runny nose and watery eyes, I give him or her Allium Cepa 12 C (Allium Cepa means onion in Latin) which is made with onion extract diluted 12 times one hundred times. It usually works very well. It is just a different way of treating, gentle and safe. If homeopathy doesn't work, then I prescribe a conventional medication.

My year of surgical training helped me tremendously in a few cases. One day, Mrs. B came to see me complaining of intense abdominal pain which had started 3 months prior. She was in her fifties, had seen several physicians already for the same abdominal pain. No physician had diagnosed anything. The last physician she saw told her she should see a psychiatrist. She was a very beautiful lady and seemed completely lost. As soon as I put my hands on her abdomen, I could tell it was a surgical abdomen. Something really bad was going on. I had to find what it was. I was thinking it could be her pancreas. Could she possibly have pancreatic cancer? She had lost a lot of weight. I sent her to the lab to get cancer markers. They were very elevated. I referred her back to her HMO doctor with a possible diagnosis of pancreatic cancer. Soon afterwards, they diagnosed her with definite pancreatic cancer. She was always very grateful to me for making the diagnosis when her other doctors had given up and were referring her to a psychiatrist. Unfortunately, by the time of her first appointment with me, her cancer was very advanced and metastasized already. Given the bad prognosis, she refused to have any treatment and passed away within 6 months.

People say, when you are a physician, you shouldn't get involved in family medical problems. Well, in the past, I always had to get involved because of medical mistakes made by other physicians. Actually, I must say that when a physician spends 5 to 15 minutes with each patient and sees 30 patients per day, he or she undoubtedly will make medical mistakes. In 10 minutes, it is impossible to examine a patient, grab the history of the disease, look at results of X-Rays, write a prescription and do this 30 times a day, 5 days a week, and make no mistake. With this mode of operation, mistakes are inevitable, since some cases are by their nature very complex.

One day, Martha, my mother- in-law called me. Joe, my father-in-law needed help. He had been diagnosed with Alzheimer's disease 6 months prior. He was taking Aricept which is an anti-Alzheimer's medication. Since he was becoming a little agitated at night, his physician had added Risperdal. Since Risperdal made him dizzy during the day, his physician switched him to Seroquel. When Martha called, she said: "Chris, I need your advice. Dad is not well. His physician started him on Seroquel 2 days ago. He was good then. Now he is unable to walk, he is hallucinating and has urinary incontinence. He is unable to eat and is drooling constantly. I am so worried. I think it is the end. He looks like he is going to die soon. What should I do?"

I was very fortunate to have a great relationship with my in laws. They were wonderful people and I adored them. I had to help them.

In reviewing Joe's history with Martha, I saw that he had lost 25 pounds in the last 6 months. Since he had never been overweight, this was a significant weight loss for him. It seemed to me that his body wasn't reacting well to either Aricept or Seroquel. I told Martha to stop all medications and I kept in touch with her calling her 2 to 3 times a day.

Within 24 hours, my father-in-law improved tremendously. Five days later he was eating well and making jokes with everybody at the table.

Even though I know I shouldn't get involved in the medical care of my family, I always end up getting involved.

Later that year, Martha called me again. That time, she was the sick one. She was coughing non-stop and had been having this dry cough for several weeks. Her physician had her on strong anti-allergy medications plus codeine which were making her very drowsy. Despite those medications, she was still coughing day and night and was getting more and more tired. I could hear her cough on the phone. Her kind of dry cough reminded me of an ACE inhibitor cough. ACE inhibitors are a kind of drug that are given to treat high blood pressure. I asked her to tell me the list of all the medications she was taking. Sure enough, in that list was an ACE inhibitor. I explained to her that it was probably the culprit. I asked her to call her physician so that he could stop her ACE inhibitor and replace it by another drug from another class. The following day, she stopped the ACE inhibitor and started another medication. Shortly after, her cough stopped and she was able to stop both the anti-allergy medications and the codeine. She quickly felt better.

This is a good example of how medications themselves can make a person sick and if this is not recognized early, physicians keep on adding more medications which have additional side effects. The end result can be a disaster and could even kill a patient.

In July 2005, I had a panic phone call from my mother in Paris. She was 83 years old then. She had had a low grade fever for one month, her blood pressure was 200 over 100 and she had a very rapid heart rate. Her physician couldn't diagnose the cause of her problem. He had given her a diuretic to lower her blood pressure but she wasn't responding to it. Blood tests and X-Rays had been done. Everything was normal except for her potassium which was very high and her sodium very low. Her physician wanted to hospitalize her but she was refusing, telling him she was allergic to hospitals. According to her, if she had to be hospitalized, she was going to die. That's how allergic to hospitals she was.

I decided to fly to Paris. I found her in bed in really bad shape with a high fever, high blood pressure, high heart rate, a dangerously low sodium level and high potassium level. She thought she was going to die. She started telling me what she wanted me to do for her funeral and said goodbye to me. I listened to her but said I would try to cure her. She told me: "Chris, you are now my doctor. Treat me the way you want but treat me at home. I am refusing to be hospitalized. If you hospitalize me, I'll die quickly."

I tried to convince her to go to the hospital, telling her that hospitals were not as bad as they used to be 50 years ago when she was younger. Now, we had very good hospitals with very good doctors. She still refused. Along my years of experience, I had come to respect such fears in patients. I had seen patients being scared to death of a particular surgery. I had seen doctors pushing for such surgery which had very little risk and to everybody's intense surprise, those patients had indeed died. I was not about to push my mother to be hospitalized. I had to respect her wishes and fears. After all, maybe she was right. We were in Paris in August again and most physicians were on vacation. Hospitals were functioning with a reduced staff. It was probably better if I could take care of her at home.

Her physician didn't want to give her any antibiotics without knowing the cause of the fever. He wanted to do a temporal artery biopsy thinking about Horton disease. As for high blood pressure treatments, he had tried several different classes of treatments but after just a few days of each one, she was developing all the side effects described in the PDR and he had to switch to another one. Right at this Moment, he was trying her on an ACE inhibitor which was making her cough day and night. The situation was a disaster.

I decided to call a few Cardiologists and Internal Medicine physicians around to get their opinion. Everybody had a different opinion of what had to be done next. I had to develop my own opinion and make my own decisions.

I decided to stop all the medications she was taking at the time and start her on a large spectrum antibiotic since we didn't know where the infection was coming from. I also started her on a different class of anti-high blood pressure medication, namely a long-acting calcium channel blocker. Since her blood sodium level was dangerously low, I bought smoked ham and salty shrimps for her. She loved that ham and shrimp diet. I also gave her a homeopathic treatment to counter the side effects of the antibiotics. After one week, both her fever and her blood pressure dropped. Her heart rate and sodium level came back to normal and we could soon stop the smoked ham and shrimp diet. She did miss those.

Two weeks later, she was back on her feet, walking everyday, eating well and making jokes. Soon afterward, I flew back to Los Angeles to take care of my patients again. I knew I had done the right thing for Mom and I felt very peaceful and warm in my heart.

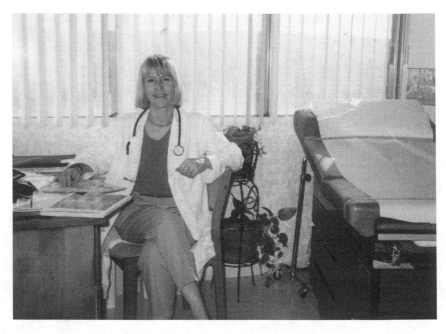

Opening my private medical practice in Torrance, California

# Chapter 24
# I need to be admitted in a hospital

When I came back to LA, I was inundated with phone calls. I had become a very popular physician. A lot of patients were happy with my way of treating them and were recommending me to their family and friends. At first, I was very flattered and tried to arrange to see as many people as I could. I started earlier in the morning and finished later at night. All my days off and my hours off had to be used for work, returning phone calls, checking laboratory results, X-ray results or doing research for difficult cases. I didn't want to refuse seeing patients so I continued adding them on to my already busy schedule. I was booked solid for one month. I was coming back home later and later every night, was getting less and less sleep and didn't have time to exercise any more. I did this for about one year. That's when I started having nightmares at night.

At first it was only one or 2 nights a week then I had terrible nightmares every night. At that time I was working on all my days off, trying to catch up with paperwork and returning 20 to 30 phone calls per day. I suddenly realized I was burnt out. I had too many patients and I wanted to take too good care of them. It was time to act and decrease my patients' load. I decided to see only alternative medicine patients and not to accept any new patient for the next month. I also decided to see fewer patients per day and finish my day at 7 or 8pm instead of 10pm. That meant I had to learn to say "no" and refer patients to other physicians if my day was too busy. This was very hard for me to do but I did it. Unfortunately it was too late. I started having acute diarrhea. At the beginning, I didn't think much of it. It was probably a viral infection. I took lots of fluids, ate lots of bananas and rice, took homeopathic medicines and continued seeing patients. One week later, since my diarrhea was still very bad, I went to see my own doctor who took stool samples and gave me antibiotics and anti-diarrhea tablets. I continued seeing patients normally. That's when the horrible happened.

Until that time, I thought I was invincible. I knew how overwork and too much stress had affected the health of some of my patients. I was actually treating a lot of them for illnesses triggered by overwork and too much stress. At one point, it becomes too much for the body and it lets us know one way or another. That's what I was teaching my patients. Well, here I was, getting caught, myself, in the exact same scenario and my body was letting me know that it was not doing the right thing!

After 2 weeks of diarrhea, despite antibiotics and anti-diarrhea tablets, when I thought it couldn't get worse, it did! My diarrhea became so profuse that I had to go every hour, day and night. Actually the days were not too bad, sometimes I only had to go every other hour during the day, but at night, it was literally every 5 minutes. I couldn't sleep any more. I was losing more that one gallon of green liquid profuse secretion per day and it was getting worse every night. There had to be something really wrong with me. The stool tests were negative for bacteria and parasites. I was now in my third week of diarrhea and couldn't drink fluids fast enough. My wonderful husband Steve was mixing several bottles of rehydration solution for me every day using one teaspoon of salt, one teaspoon of baking soda and 7 teaspoons of sugar for one liter of water. Despite this, I was getting dehydrated and having electrolytes imbalance. I was getting more and more tired everyday. I needed IV fluids! I needed a specialist to take care of me and find the origin of this diarrhea! I tried seeing patients one more day, hoping the symptoms would miraculously disappear. They didn't. The following morning, I was being admitted at the hospital.

That's when it seemed that my life stopped. I wasn't a physician anymore. I was a patient in a hospital bed. I had several nurses around me trying to get an IV access to give me fluids and potassium intravenously.

Unfortunately, I was so dehydrated that they couldn't find any good vein. Once they would find one and stick it with a needle, it would instantaneously blow. Several nurses tried several times. Pretty soon, I was screaming with pain, my hands and wrists covered with hematomas and I still didn't have an IV access. Yes, I had indeed become a patient. I had become a body, a very sick body which had to run to the bathroom every 15 minutes for a profuse diarrhea. I was miserable!

Finally, the hospital staff called a very experienced nurse to stick me. She managed to find an IV access and soon, fluids flowed into my body at 150cc an hour. I felt relieved. I didn't have to drink gallons of my special rehydration solution any more. My stomach could finally rest.

The infectious disease specialist came to see me. I was hopeful that he would find the origin of my diarrhea and treat it appropriately. Maybe in a few days, I would be all back to normal. Unfortunately, after hearing my story and examining me, he concluded that my problem was not infectious. He ordered a few cancer tests and called a gastroenterologist to take over. That's when I started to worry about my condition. I had brought all my medical books and I looked at all the non-infectious origins of secretory diarrhea. There were several cancers listed among those, colon cancer, pancreatic cancer, vipomas and carcinoid tumors. I had horrible flashbacks of my Dad's fight against colon cancer. I became horribly depressed, imagining the worst and thinking about death.

The gastroenterologist came. She was a very nice doctor but also a very pregnant lady. What she said didn't reassure me much. She said I needed a complete work-up. She planned for a colonoscopy with biopsies+ an upper endoscopy + abdomen and pelvis CT scan for the following day. The next 2 days were hell for me. I really thought I was going to die. I wasn't eating anything any more and still liters and liters of fluids were coming out of my behind. I was losing weight very fast and looked like a skeleton. I became convinced I had some kind of incurable advanced cancer. I was so weak that I thought I would be unable to go through surgery and chemotherapy if I had to. My life had stopped. I started reviewing my life, thanking God for all the good years I had and getting mentally ready for death. Nothing mattered any more. Steve was juggling his work and spending as much time with me as he could. The only thing I could do was cry on his shoulder and in his arms. I was crying non stop. I was at the end of my rope. I was at the end of what my body could take! I was ready for death!

It is fascinating to see how quickly things can deteriorate. Three weeks before, I was this very successful invincible physician. Three sleepless weeks later and gallons of diarrhea later, I was this very sick body with only bone and skin left, hiding in a hospital bed and getting ready for death. At 7:00 am the following day, after another sleepless night with a lot of diarrhea, I started having very severe abdominal cramps. They were so painful that my nurse had to give me my first Morphine IV shot. The effect was immediate. The pain completely stopped in 3 minutes and I started being in a daze. I thought about all the IV Morphine addicts. So this is the feeling they are looking for! I said to myself. Well their life must be really bad if such a feeling of daze makes them so happy and addicted. For me, the daze didn't feel good. I liked the feeling of real life better, but it sure did the job of killing the pain.

At 8:00 am the hospital staff took me to the endoscopy suite for an upper and lower endoscopy with biopsies, then in the afternoon the same day, they took me to the radiology department for a CT scan. The radiology technician used my very small IV access in my right hand to inject contrast at a high speed. It started burning terribly. I screamed and screamed in pain, asking him to stop but he relentlessly kept on injecting the contrast. I knew my vein was too small to use for IV contrast but I couldn't do anything. I was hopeless. I was just an average patient. I had to suffer. When I came back to my room after the day full of procedures, I was bleeding from my colon from all the biopsies taken, my hand was swollen and very painful after the burn from the IV contrast and I still had my relentless diarrhea. I was falling lower and lower. Death was getting closer and closer. Time had stopped. There were no days and nights any more. I was waiting for the verdict. I was waiting for the diagnosis. In fact, I wasn't sure I wanted to know my diagnosis. I was afraid to have my very little one per cent chance of survival disappear.

I decided that if there were metastasis everywhere I wouldn't go through surgery or chemotherapy but that I would enjoy my last days with Steve and my mother, then die quickly. I was mentally ready.

On the other hand, I promised myself that if the diagnosis was benign, if my condition was treatable and if I eventually was to get back to normal, my way of practicing medicine would change. I would see less patients per day, making sure to spend quality time with all of my patients for them but also for my personal fulfillment. I would never let myself become overwhelmed again by work, phone calls and paperwork. I realized that money is not that important. What is important is happiness. I needed to be happy. True happiness was giving my body strength and health. Now I had neither and I was miserable.

Two hours later, my gastroenterologist came to see me: "Dr. Gilbert, we have a diagnosis. Two biopsies came back positive." My heart stopped. That was it. That was probably my death sentence. I prepared myself mentally for the bad news. All my muscles tensed up. "You have lymphocytic colitis" she continued. The name was vaguely familiar. I asked her to explain what it was. "It is not cancer. It is an inflammation of the bowel. Your small intestine isn't working any more. It is secreting fluids instead of absorbing nutrients. Your large bowel isn't absorbing water any more like it should. It is a rare but curable condition. Unfortunately it could take some time to get back to normal. 95% of people in your condition react well to Pepto-Bismol within 1 to 2 months. I'll start you on Pepto-Bismol right now."

"What about my CT scan?" I asked, shaking, imagining metastasis everywhere. She replied that my CT scan was normal and left the room.

Left alone, I started sobbing and sobbing and sobbing, overwhelmed by the emotion. I couldn't believe it! I didn't have cancer! I didn't need surgery! I didn't need chemotherapy or radiation therapy! This was the best news ever! This was the best possible scenario! I couldn't have wished for anything better. I felt blessed. I lay down on my hospital bed, breathing deeply and thanking God and my Dad who had become my guardian angel.

# Chapter 25
# True Happiness

## *January 2007*

It took me 3 long months to slowly get back on my feet. My normal weight was 108 lbs but when I left the hospital, I was 88 lbs. 88 lbs for 5'4" wasn't much! When I had clothes on, I looked like a model but naked, I looked like a skeleton. The diarrhea took a long time to resolve. Pepto-Bismol didn't work. I had to take Asacol which worked a little bit but not enough. I had to add steroids and drink gallons of potassium. After 3 months, the abdominal pain and diarrhea finally resolved.

I started work again, remembering the promise I had made to myself if I was going to come out of this alive and well: I needed to enjoy every single minute of the rest of my life.

It would have been very easy to do like most physicians do in LA: spend less time with each patient and see more patients per day. I refused to do this. My practice had to remain a quality one where each of my patients was special. I did consider them as my children, all of them. I spent one hour with each patient, making sure I was addressing all his or her questions and fears. I double checked that they are eating, drinking and exercising the right way. I prescribed homeopathy first and used acupuncture when appropriate. Only if the patient really needed them, did I prescribe conventional medications. A lot of conventional medications come with significant side effects and I tried to minimize that. I wanted to remain their family doctor, which meant being part of my patients' family and them being part of mine. This was incredibly rewarding. Hearing my patients thank me from the bottom of their hearts was worth every single minute I spent with them. It provided me with an intense feeling of fulfillment and gave meaning to my life.

I also remained committed to my love of show business. If a TV production called for me to be on a TV show, I immediately accepted. My patients knew that, after what I had gone through, my main purpose was to enjoy life, to enjoy every minute of being on a TV show, to enjoy every single minute spent helping them, to enjoy every single minute spent with my loving husband Steve, my wonderful mother and the rest of my extended family and friends. I was not forcing myself to do things anymore. It felt like the old Dr. Chris Gilbert had died on that hospital bed when she was having acute diarrhea. A new Dr. Chris was born and this one was radiant with happiness, taking nothing for granted any more. I was happy to be alive, I was healthier than ever before and appreciated every single minute of this very precious life I had been given. From time to time, I needed to pause and lie down. There, I would take a few deep breaths, would become aware of my lungs working perfectly, would listen to the regular music of my heart beat, would make each muscle and joint of my body move pain free. It was such an intense pleasure to rediscover all those qualities that we take for granted. They are real miracles and I appreciated them as such.

The year 2007 was delightful! Steve and I appreciated every second of our healthy and happy life together! Wonderful meals! Wonderful love making! When we thought it couldn't get any better, it got better! He was truly my soul mate, my Prince Charming, the Love of my Life. In 11 years of marriage, we hadn't argued, not even once! Steve's sense of humor was wonderful and turned every day into a magical one.

We decided to celebrate our 11 year anniversary in Thailand. It was the most wonderful trip we ever took! I had reserved the best hotels in Bangkok, Koh Samui, Phuket and Chiang Mai. The trip lasted 3 wonderful weeks. We took elephant rides in rivers, went kayaking around the islands and caves of the Phang Gna Bay, snorkeled near the

Phi Phi islands, sailed catamarans, played chess on the beach and had the most romantic and colorful breakfasts and dinners. We did live those 3 weeks as if there were no tomorrow and enjoyed every second of them. We brought back a whole suitcase full of presents for family and friends.

One month after coming back to LA, we flew Steve's Mom, Martha from Pennsylvania to LA and took her on her dream trip to Las Vegas, Palm Springs and San Francisco. There too, we reserved the best Las Vegas Suite in the one of the best Hotels on the strip, went to the best shows and tried to make Martha as happy and fulfilled as possible. We all enjoyed every single second of our trip.

I had succeeded in my goal. I was cherishing every single second of my precious life.

Our last trip together in Thailand

# Chapter 26
## Living the unimaginable

In January 2008, my Mom came to visit from Paris and I decided to take her on her dream Island Maui, Hawaii during the time Steve was on business trip. That's when the unimaginable happened.

As Mom and I were in Maui for 5 days, Steve called me from Colorado. He was worried about his right hand. Its typing speed was becoming slower than his left hand's. I told him to go to Urgent Care and see a doctor there. He decided to wait thinking it was Carpel Tunnel Syndrome.

Twenty four hours later, he called me again, letting me know that his right hand was getting worse. It was typing even slower. He still postponed an Urgent Care visit, thinking he would be back in LA soon.

The following day, as he was flying back into LA, he went to Urgent Care. His doctor diagnosed a possible beginning of stroke and offered to hospitalize him. He refused, choosing instead to have a Brain MRI done the following week.

A few hours later, Mom and I landed in LA. I immediately examined Steve and what I found horrified me: Not only could he not move his right fingers any more but he was starting to lose sensitivity of his right shoulder and his right hip. In my mind, only one thing could give those exact same symptoms: a brain tumor! I tried to get this diagnosis out of my mind, thinking I was probably over diagnosing. I took Steve to the emergency room right away. As he was in the waiting room, waiting to have a Brain MRI, suddenly he started screaming, looking at his right hand. All the muscles of his right hand and fingers started contracting and shaking with intense pain. It was unbearable to watch! It was as if the hand which was almost paralyzed before, was starting to have a life of its own, uncontrollable, scary. As Steve was completely panicking, he was taken straight to the Emergency room again. He had just had his first focal seizure!

From then on, things went downhill very fast. An urgent brain MRI showed a large brain tumor imbedded in the most precious part of his left brain: the motor strip responsible for all movements of the right part of the body and also imbedded in the speech area. It was a disaster! It was the worse possible case scenario! I was still hoping that the tumor was benign but 5 days later when the neurosurgeon tried to remove it, the exact diagnosis showed up: Glioblastoma multiforme, the most aggressive fast growing incurable brain cancer on the planet! The cancer cells were so untangled with the healthy cells responsible for speech and for the movement of his right fingers that removing them would have left him paralyzed from his right hand and probably unable to speak. He decided to not have the tumor removed. The verdict was severe. Steve had between 6 months (best case scenario) to 3 years (best case scenario) to live but most probably less than one year. We were devastated!

From that day on, our lives changed drastically! No more plans for the future to grow old together, retire together and buy a new house on a bigger land!

It all changed to planning for radiation therapy, chemotherapy, exploring new clinical trials with new vaccines, new drugs to fight GBM (glioblastoma multiforme). I tried to get Steve in the best and most promising clinical trials but none of them would accept him. His tumor was too big!

With the help of several of the best physicians in town, we managed to shrink the tumor and Steve managed to have full use of his right fingers again. Steroids, radiation therapy and chemotherapy (it was chemotherapy in the form of oral pills, we were lucky) combined were successful! We started living a little again. Unfortunately, we had to battle severe side effects of radiation therapy, steroids and chemo. Steve was so tired all the time (radiation therapy). He started gaining a lot of fat and losing a lot of muscle (steroids), having high blood pressure (steroids), diabetes (steroids), cataract in both eyes (steroids), swollen legs (steroids), shortness of breath (combination of steroids and chemo) abdominal pain (chemo). In addition to all those side effects, he was still battling frequent focal seizures that would come all of a sudden, most often after the slightest effort. First his right thumb and index finger would twitch then his whole hand would get into a horrible spasm that would make him scream, then the spasms would come to the right part of his face then to the speech area. Each seizure would last less than 3 minutes but it was spectacular. Each time a seizure would start, I would run to him to place a little piece of Lorazepam(anti-seizure medication) under his tongue to decrease the intensity of the seizure. I would also hold his arm firmly to decrease the pain from spasms and I would stay with him and hold him. One day as I was downstairs, I heard a loud "boom" upstairs as if something heavy had just fallen. I run upstairs and found Steve on the floor, seizing from the whole right side of his body, twitching from his face and unable to speak. That seizure lasted a long time, more than 5 minutes, even with the Lorazepam and scared both of us.

Hell had begun! I started getting very depressed! Amazingly enough, Steve never got depressed. He was frequently asking: "Why me? Was I bad?" I would answer: "No, my Love, you are the best and most wonderful man on earth! You always think about everybody else before yourself and want to make everybody happy around you! I love you so much! You shouldn't have to go through this! This isn't fair!" After hearing this, he would smile and kiss me. I was in awe at how he handled the situation. All his efforts were into trying to survive another day, another week, another month and organizing all the 15 different medications he had to take everyday. He was frequently on the computer, updating his charts showing the intensity of his symptoms and his different medications. He never gave up and was always fighting, never depressed, just very tired.

I frequently asked myself: "Why us?" So many couples didn't get along and argued all the time. Yet nothing happened to them and they lived into their 80's. So many people were "bad" people and yet nothing was happening to them. Here we were so happy together, Steve was 55 years old, still young and very handsome, always doing the best he could for everybody else and being a true really good man. Life was really not fair!

Three months after Steve's diagnosis, another really good man Senator Ted Kennedy was diagnosed with the same type of cancer. We didn't feel alone any more. Senator Ted Kennedy and his family had just become part of ours without them knowing it. We started comparing treatments (which were very similar) and side effects that we could see. Steve got the same quality of care I think, as Senator Kennedy, which means he got the best possible treatments. Vicky Kennedy, if you ever get to read this book, know that we lived the same experience at about the same time and about the same age: a wonderful marriage then a dreadful diagnosis for our most perfect husband, then the same fight for life at the same time. I felt very close to you for many months. Your life was in the spotlight, my life was in the dark but our hearts were beating in unison.

One year after the diagnosis, as we were rejoicing that the tumor was still at bay, that Steve was still alive when most people after one year were dead, the most recent brain MRI showed a change. The tumor was starting to grow again. We had to change chemo, start IV infusions. At the same time, Steve's cataract was so severe in both eyes that he had to undergo cataract surgery, 2 different surgeries, 2 weeks apart. He also had to have a port-a-cath placed under the clavicle to have an easy IV access for regular IV chemo every 2 weeks.

Steve handled every surgery and every treatment with incredible courage, never complaining, always trying to survive the next day, the next week, the next month. I, on the other hand, started to be more and more depressed. I was crying very often but yet I was trying to not show my depression to Steve. What was going on? He was the sick one and I was the depressed one? That didn't make sense! I had to come back to my senses and be the strong one! Yet I couldn't! I was seeing him every day fighting for his life, seeing him every day getting weaker and weaker, suffering more and more, having more and more side effects. The slow downhill ride became unbearable to watch. He started having more and more abdominal pain (due to the new IV chemo), more and more shortness of breath sometimes only at rest. I tried getting very busy, washing clothes, cooking for him, helping him with his meds, doctors visits etc... Nothing would work.

It is OK to be a physician and tell people to take such and such drug and to fight for their life. It is another story when I am the wife of my beloved husband, the most wonderful man on earth and when I have to watch him suffer every day 24 hours a day for months and months, slowly going downhill, slowly suffering more every day, yet trying to remain the most wonderful loving husband. It was like living in a torture chamber 24 hours a day watching the man I loved being tortured again and again, falling on his knees, getting up again, being tortured again, falling on his knees, getting up again... It was unbearable! Yet it was Steve's decision to continue with a very hard chemo until he couldn't fight any more. I had to respect his decision. I was trying to be his loving wife but also his doctor, his nurse, his physical therapist and his taxi driver. I couldn't work anymore. I became so depressed that I thought about killing myself. I had to call my best friend who is a psychiatrist for help. That is when I started needing breaks and decided to call Steve's sisters to help.

On 2 different occasions, Steve had near death experiences. The first time was shortly after his diagnosis when his brain was swelling very rapidly from the tumor growth. He described seeing dancing fountains and hearing a certain drum tempo that was calling him. Fortunately with the help of IV steroids, we managed to reduce his brain swelling and bring him back to life. The second time was when after one year, his tumor started growing again and his brain started swelling again. There again, he described the same dancing fountains and hearing the same drum tempo that was calling him. Again, we managed to reduce the swelling and he came back to life. Those dancing fountains and this precise drum tempo made a profound impression on him both times. He never forgot those.

We said goodbye many times and I will always be grateful for this. Having the time to say goodbye is priceless. We told each other many times how much we loved each other, how much the 12 years living together were the best years of our life, how much we changed each other's life for the best, how much we would always love each other even if death was going to take us apart. Our eyes would always shed tears as we would cuddle, feeling our intense, deep and perfect love for each other.

First we said goodbye just before his brain surgery since we didn't know if he was going to get out of the surgery room alive. Then we said goodbye 10 days after the surgery when he was having a lot of seizures and thought he was going to die. One year later, we said goodbye when the tumor started growing again. He promised that if he could, he would send me signs from Heaven or wherever he was.

As time went by, Steve's focal seizures decreased in intensity. After one year and 2 months, they became a non issue with just a few painless spasms in his right thumb. That was a big relief.

The second line chemo, the IV stuff, worked well and stopped the tumor from growing again. We were thankful. The only problem is that as time went by, Steve would have more and more side effects. Since most of his hair fell, he started growing a beard which turned white and started falling also. Then his abdominal pain and shortness of breath increased. We took numerous trips to the Emergency Room. They couldn't find any cause other than chemo.

We decided to take a last trip. I went to Paris to see my elderly mother who was feeling very dizzy and was worried about her health (she had turned 86 years old and I hadn't seen her in one year) while Steve went to Pennsylvania to see his mother, brothers and sisters. He spent a good week there then his sister Barbie flew back with him to California.

One day after their flying back to LA, Steve's abdominal pain took a turn for the worse. His pain was so intense that Barbie called 911 and got him hospitalized. I flew back to LA.

# Chapter 27
## Steve goes to Heaven

I went from Paris airport to LA and directly to Steve's hospital room. I found him with pneumonia, coughing a lot, short of breath even on oxygen, and with intense abdominal pain. This didn't look good. My heart broke! What were we going to do? Could we stop all this pain and suffering? Could we get him back to normal? Barbie was at his side, Joe his brother was also there and Joey, Joe's son, our nephew was due to arrive the following day.

Barbie had stayed with Steve night and day for several days and was exhausted. She had to fly back to Pennsylvania. With Joe and Joey we organized a 24 hour watch. Mostly Joe and Joey stayed with Steve at night and I stayed with him during the days.

I called all the specialists (lung, gastroenterologist, infectious disease, internal medicine and oncologist). During 5 days, we battled with higher doses of oxygen and potent antibiotics. We did all the CT scans and MRI needed. A CT scan of the chest and abdomen found small pockets of fluid in his abdomen. One was drained. No bacteria was found. Was it a virus? Steve's lungs couldn't absorb oxygen any more! He was getting short of breath even with the highest dose of oxygen! Why? Was it a side effect of chemo? Was it a virus? A new brain MRI unfortunately showed that the tumor had started growing again despite very aggressive IV chemo. That is when I knew that we had lost the battle.

For a couple of days, I managed to get Steve better. The antibiotics were working on the pneumonia and he was coughing less, being more comfortable and having less abdominal pain. He still needed a lot of oxygen. During those 2 days, in our hospital private room, we cuddled, said how much we loved each other, how much our years together had been the most wonderful of our lives and reminisced. He also confirmed that he didn't want to be on any ventilator nor did he want to have his life prolonged if there was no normal life in sight. We shed tears in each other arms fully appreciating each other's presence and embrace.

The following morning, he started having intense abdominal pain and being short of breath again on maximum oxygen. That is when I decided to put him on a Morphine drip which made his last day very peaceful with Joe, Joey and I by his side.

He stopped breathing many times that day with me holding his hand then finally, at 10:00 pm on June 23rd, Steve went to Heaven.

Joe, Joey and I held each other, eyes full of tears then we took deep breaths and called the medical team.

# Chapter 28
## Steve's funeral

I needed to grieve. I needed to stay by myself and cry for many days. I couldn't do any of those. Modern civilization is so hard. I had to organize Steve's funeral, choose a suit for him to wear in Heaven, sign papers, address bank accounts problems etc.... Finally I understood what my mother went through when my father died. I never understood it fully until that exact moment.

I flew Steve's body to Pittsburgh, Pennsylvania where Martha, my mother-in-law had bought a cemetery space for both of us. I flew myself to Pittsburgh where Barbie, my sister-in-law and Denny her husband picked me up. I stayed with them for a week, not knowing exactly who I was any more. I had to choose a casket, cards, flowers etc…that was real torture.

Barbie and Denny owned an alpaca farm and I found comfort spending hours with their beautiful animals. Steve and I had gone numerous times and I had helped delivered several baby alpacas. The very first one I helped delivered was Jack, a gorgeous cream-colored male who would always run to me to greet me. That had always been one of the highlights of my Pennsylvania trips. This time, I couldn't spend much time with humans. I had to either be by myself crying or with the alpacas thinking. I needed to go back to nature.

Then came "viewing day". I wanted to go in by myself first and have some time alone with Steve. When I entered the room, I was shocked.

The room was full of flowers that many people had sent from all over the United States. The most beautiful flowers, white, pink, orange, many plants and even tapestries…. In the middle of those, Steve was lying in a beautiful casket with a white satin interior, wearing his favorite suit, his favorite tie, shirt and shoes. What an unreal vision! I slowly approached. Tears came to my eyes. He looked so peaceful, beautiful, almost smiling. Like I did for my Dad, I checked that his legs and feet were resting the right way so that his body wouldn't be hurt. I touched his face, the contour of his nose, his mouth, his forehead to engrave those in my mind. Here was the man who made me so happy for so many years. He was the Love of my Life, who I would never find ever again on this Earth. He was my Perfect match. Who was I without him? What would I do without him? How can I survive without him? More tears came to my eyes, lots of tears. After what seemed like eternity, I came back to my senses and went back into the other room where the family was. That is when real viewing day started.

Viewing day was one of the most horrible days of my entire life. In France, viewings don't exist. Now I know why. It was horrible to see Steve's body lying in an open casket and have a lot of people come to me, tell me "I am sorry for your loss" (I came to hate that sentence) then go to him, pay their respect, then stay around and talk to each other. This lasted several hours, several very long hours. I don't know how I managed to go through it but somehow I managed.

The nice thing is that so many people came, so many friends and family, so many people that I knew but also so many people I didn't know. People who knew him when he was a child, and also work colleagues who traveled several hundred miles to be with us and described how wonderful and perfect Steve's work was and how wonderful a person he was.

The following morning was the funeral. A few minutes were spent at the funeral home where I touched Steve's skin, nose, cheeks and lips again for the last time. I couldn't get enough of touching his skin, although it was cold and solid as stone, it was still the skin of the Love of my Life. It was still his face, face that had made me laugh so many times, face that had loved me so much for 13 years. I touched him one last time then the casket closed and we went on our way to the Catholic Church in Bentleyville for the most wonderful and personal mass, said by the most wonderful priest I had ever seen, then to the cemetery in Beallsville. That is when Steve sent me the first sign.

Somehow, Steve's soul was communicating with me. I knew it. Just like my Dad's soul communicated with me shortly after his death: The day of my Dad's funeral, the sky was grey but nice. As we started to bury him, it started raining. As my Mom and I left the cemetery, it stopped raining. I found it strange but thought nothing of it. One week later, as it was a beautiful day, we went to the cemetery again. As we arrived close to the cemetery, out of the blue, clouds came. By the time we arrived near the grave, black clouds were over our head. When we started talking to Dad, it started raining. When we left the cemetery, the rain stopped. That was more than strange. I took it as a sign from Dad's soul telling us, he was there with us, crying with us, missing us but also looking over us and protecting us.

Well, guess what happened at Steve's funeral! It was a grey day but no rain. As soon as we arrived at the grave site to bury him, it started raining and even pouring…I took it as a sign again! I knew then that he was there, already up there, crying so much with us, missing us so much but also looking over us and committed to protect us.

Three days later, as it was a beautiful weather, we went on Steve's grave again. As we arrived on his grave, covered with beautiful flowers, it didn't rain. As I was kneeling down on his grave, I looked up in the sky. The sky had become grey. One single big black cloud was over his grave. It was centered right over the grave. It was beautiful. It was going to rain. My heart almost stopped and tears poured from my eyes. Steve was not down under any more. He was right there over my head, so close, almost looking at me in the eyes, looking over me and protecting me. He was here, I knew it, I could feel him. I stopped looking down and talking to the grave. I started looking up and talking to the cloud. It was so beautiful, so elegant, so black. It didn't rain…It didn't have to…

The week in Pennsylvania was the most difficult week of my entire life! Fortunately I had the help and support of Steve's family. A lot of help and support!

Then everything was over and everybody went back home. Life started again for everybody. They started living again and joking again. That is when I understood what grieving really was. How was I supposed to live again, laugh again like everybody else? I couldn't! Everybody else had their own life still intact. I didn't! My life had changed drastically. I had lost the man I was living for, my "raison d'etre". I had lost the most precious person in my life, the one who was giving me a purpose in life. I couldn't live again and joke again like everybody else. I had to fly back to California to be by myself and grieve.

With my favorite alpacas

# Chapter 29
# Flying back to California… ALONE

When I arrived at LAX, nobody was waiting for me at the airport. This was so new! Usually, either Steve was traveling with me or he would come to the airport to pick me up. This was my first shock. I took a cab and arrived at the house. There, I was still hoping to see Steve come out of the house and greet me but he didn't. The house was empty. I went to Steve's desk in his home office then to our bedroom. Nobody! The house was just like he left it, with his clothes everywhere, lots of medications everywhere, computers, monitors, amateur radios, radio controlled helicopters, tools, lots of tools, cars, his 3 cars. The house was still as if he was still there and yet… I collapsed crying and went to bed.

The following days, I tried keeping myself busy with mail and work. I couldn't touch any of Steve's things. I left everything everywhere.

One month later, 4 of Steve's colleagues came to clean up his home office and take computers, files and CD that belonged to the company. That was so hard for me to watch!

Two months later Steve's 2 sisters and 2 brothers arrived for the weekend. Then and then only, we started putting his clothes and things in plastic containers and put them in the garage. I was devastated and yet, this had to be done. Two rooms and the garage were completely filled with stuff. They were so many items that it was almost impossible to get into those rooms. Most doors of the house had been taken off and had been replaced by hangers hanging Steve's numerous and beautiful work shirts. All the corridors were covered with things acquired along the years. The house was a mess. Thanks to Steve's brothers and sisters, one of the rooms became usable and I made it my new office. The backyard quickly filled up with to-be-thrown-away things. The family put doors again in most of the rooms. The house was already transformed a little. It looked much better. There were still a lot of boxes of papers I would have to go through in the years to come but half of the work had been done. I cried a lot that week-end.

Then everybody left and I remained by myself again. A lot of paperwork had been done and I was a little less busy with my private practice. This meant I had more time to think.

Then came questions again. Who am I without Steve? What is my goal in life? What do I want to do in the next few years? Who am I living for? Who am I working for? I had no answer for any of those questions. They were so foreign to me! The reality hit me! *There was no future I could see without Steve. I was lost.*

# Chapter 30
## Staying in my cave and cocooning.

There was no future I could see for myself. As for the past, it was too painful to remember. There was only one thing left for me to do: be in the Present. At first, I couldn't see much in my present and then, little by little, I saw more and more.

I started being aware of the ground, solid under my feet. I lied down on the grass, face down, arms extended, feeling the earth with my whole body and touching the grass with my fingers. It felt good. Everything and everybody dear to my heart could be taken away from me but not this. This Mother Earth could never be taken away from me. It felt so reassuring. I started taking long walks outside, listening to birds, looking at squirrels, looking at all the flowers on my walks, stopping to smell them and looking at the sky. I had pleasure from embracing trees, feeling how strong trunks were, feeling the texture of the bark, inhaling to get some of this strength inside of me. I had no more hugs from Steve but hugging trees became a huge support. I loved one particular tree which trunk was way too big for me to embrace with my arms. It had huge roots and beautiful branches and leaves. It became my anchor and my source of strength. Nothing else but nature existed. It was just the "here and now", just the present minute, just the present second. I started to come back to life and to my senses.

I spent time at the beach, touching the sand, looking at the ocean and spotting some dolphins. I started kayaking again, admiring the beauty of the pelicans and the playfulness of the seals, appreciating the warmth of the sun on my skin and the sound of the waves.

At home, I took out of the cupboard my most beautiful China, silver silverware and crystal glasses and started using them for special meals I cooked for myself. I cut fresh flowers everyday and put them on the dining room table. I got out my most beautiful candles and started lighting them every night for dinner. I started living in the Moment and for the Present Moment. That Moment was my present, past and future. There was nothing else. *I was completely empty.*

Slowly, day after day, week after week, month after month, this complete emptiness I was feeling inside started changing. My heart and my soul started filling up with all the beauty from Mother Nature. I little by little started feeling very full, full of beauty and love.

I started remembering all the wonderful moments Steve and I had spent together and felt very grateful for the 12 wonderful years of marriage we had. I knew what a happy and perfect marriage was. I was so fortunate! So many people spend their entire life looking for this and never find it. I felt blessed and so full of the love from our marriage.

I also spent a lot of time with our cat, Maui. Maui appeared in my life the day I moved in with Steve. She was just a few weeks old and belonged to the next door neighbor. She was all black, with a very soft fur, had white whiskers, bright yellow eyes and a very loud voice. As Steve and I would play table tennis in the backyard, she would love to come and run after the white ball. Later she started scratching our side door to come in the house or ask for food or water. For some reason, she didn't like it next door (her official home). Before long, she started scratching the door more and more often meowing very loudly… That's when we named her Maui because she was meowing so much and so loudly. When the next door neighbor moved out, he asked us if we wanted to keep her. Steve loved cats just like his dad did so we said yes. That's how Maui came into my life. After Steve passing, she became my little support. We would cuddle for hours. She loved that. She needed to be with me and touch me all the time. She followed me everywhere

189

My cat Maui

like a little doggy. Our favorite moment was at night when watching TV or reading medical magazines in the living room, I would lie down on the floor and she would come on my chest, lick my nose then lie on my heart, facing me, her two front paws embracing me on each side of my chest. We would stay like this for hours, purring with comfort. That was good for both of us.

I was still seeing patients in the office and I started going to a "transition group" on Monday nights. That was enough for my social life. The rest of the time, I didn't want to see anybody. I was comfortable by myself. I started writing and adding the last chapters to this book.

Staying in my cave and cocooning had become increasingly pleasurable. I was making all my senses work. I was more aware of nature, its beauty, its smells, sounds and touch. I became more in tune with myself and in harmony with my body and the universe.

That's when I received signs from Steve from Heaven…

# Chapter 31
## Signs from Steve from Heaven.

I am a physician and my brain is very logical. I don't believe in signs from Heaven and I was never looking for those signs, yet, what happened changed all my beliefs.

Two weeks after Steve's death, as I was lying in bed at night, my right thumb and index finger started shaking uncontrollably. I got very worried and thought I was getting a brain tumor too. Or was it a sign from Steve, telling me his soul was with me? He used to have seizures that would start with the exact same 2 fingers shaking. It was such an incredible coincidence. I tried to relax. Nothing stopped the shaking. Finally, after one hour or so, I managed to fall asleep. In the morning, when I woke up, I had forgotten all about it when suddenly the shaking started again. Medically, it was a resting tremor of only those 2 fingers. I went to the office and as I was talking to patients, I had to hide my right hand under my desk because my thumb and forefinger were shaking nonstop. Every night, I started talking to Steve when the tremor would get more intense. I told him that I knew it was him causing the shaking to let me know that he was there close to me, looking over me and protecting me. I told him how much I loved him, how much I would always love him, how I knew I would never ever find again in this life time anybody as wonderful as him, as perfect for me as him, how much I missed him, the same way he probably missed me. Then I would go to bed, still shaking and wake up the following day, still shaking. I decided to wait a few days before seeing any physician. If it was a bad diagnosis, things would get worse. If it was a sign from Steve, things would improve. The tremor lasted one week, one whole week! Then, day after day, it slowly decreased and after 2 weeks it completely stopped without any medication. I took it as a sign from Steve from Heaven.

One month after Steve's death, as I was walking from my office to the hospital for my usual lunch break, I suddenly spotted a red balloon flying over my head. It was heart-shaped. I turned around to see who it belonged to but couldn't find anybody. The surroundings were empty. My heart started pounding. Could it be from Steve? I didn't want to think about that and continued walking, trying to ignore the balloon. This quickly became impossible as this beautiful red heart balloon started flying ahead of me, right in front of my face and landed in between my 2 feet, forcing me to pick it up. I turned around again to see if anybody was there. The streets were empty. There was nobody else but me. Tears started flowing out of my eyes. I looked up at the sky and talked to Steve to thank him. Steve used to frequently offer me such balloons…

Two months after his death, I decided to give one of his cars to his sister Barbie. We went to the DMV. The car's license plate was SAC1, which stands for Strategic Air Command 1 or Steve A. Chmura 1 which were Steve's initials. It was Steve's favorite license plate. On another car, he had SAC2, and the 3rd one, SAC4. In the middle of the transaction, the DMV person asked me if I wanted to keep the SAC1 plate or release it to the public. I debated it. I knew it was Steve's favorite license plate but would I use it? Probably not! I decided to release it to the public. The very moment I said so, all the computers at the DMV froze! There was an announcement overhead saying that the DMV had just experienced computer problems and everything had to be on standby until the problem could be fixed. Everybody had to sit down and wait. I was stunned! I knew Steve was an excellent computer engineer. He could do anything and everything with computers, electricity, plumbing, everything! Could this be a sign from him telling me to keep his favorite license plate? I couldn't believe that. I talked to Barbie about that. We agreed that it could be a sign from him. I still decided to release the license plate to the public. The computers remained out of order. We continued to sit there waiting. Finally, I had enough! If this was a sign from Steve, I had to respect it. I decided to get a new form and agreed to keep his favorite license plate. As I was signing it, the DMV computers started working again! Barbie and I were stunned. I was smiling, trying to imagine his soul, playing with the DMV computers, trying to give me the message to keep his SAC1. Steve was so bright and so inventive! He could do anything! I loved him so much! Barbie and I left the DMV, full of love for Steve. We talked to him on the way back, telling him we respected his wishes and kept his favorite license plate. We could imagine him smiling in Heaven.

A few days later, one of Steve's friends brought somebody to look at his model helicopters and planes to maybe buy them. As we were in the garage, looking at them and discussing prices, the light over the helicopters and over us suddenly shut off by itself. Again, I was stunned. All the other lights in the garage were still on. Only this one was off! Was it a sign from Steve? Did he want me to keep his helicopters and planes? Or was I asking too high of a price? I didn't know. Anyhow, after 10 minutes, we decided to get back in the house. That's when the lights turned on again by themselves. I decided to keep the helicopters and planes for now.

Steve hated when I had a hair perm and cut. He liked me with long straight hair.

Well, since he wasn't around anymore, at least not down here on earth, I decided to get a new look and get a hair perm and cut. I made an appointment with my favorite hairdresser. I'll call her Diana, in order to protect her real name. Diana had cut Steve's hair once and knew how wonderful a man he was. She had been cutting my hair for the last 7 years. The day of the appointment, she started putting my hair in small curlers. After rolling a few, she looked for pins to hold the curlers together. To her huge surprise, she couldn't find any. She opened all the drawers and cupboards. As she did so, she got very nervous and boxes started falling down on the floor. I had my eyes wide open and smiled. Could it be a sign from Steve? I knew he really hated perms and short hair...I started laughing. I must admit that things were very comical. Diana was now completely lost. All the cupboards were opened and most boxes had fallen on the floor making a real mess. Diana was saying, talking to herself: "I don't understand, I usually find at least a few pins here and there but now, I cannot find any. This is so incredible." Then talking to me: "I am so sorry Dr. Gilbert, we might have to reschedule." Amused, I told her I could reschedule for 3 days later. We set a new appointment and as I left her hair salon, I thought that if it was a sign from Steve, he would find a way for the perm not to happen in 3 days. I was curious to see what he would do. I came back home full of love for Steve.

Three days later, as I was waking up, the phone rang. Guess who? It was Diana! Her voice was so hoarse I could barely recognize it. She was sick in bed with a fever and sore throat. She was so sorry she had to cancel my appointment. I told her not to worry and to take care of herself. As I hang up the phone, I smiled. Steve had found a way! He was so wonderful!

Then I went to France to spend 2 and half weeks with my mother. I went there with straight long hair, just like what Steve liked. When I came back, I decided to make another appointment with Diana... for again a perm and a cut...I was really looking forward to that perm and fresh cut. The day before the appointment, Diana called to tell me that everything was in order and ready for me the following day. This time, nothing would stop her. I smiled and thanked her. The day of the appointment, I was surprised that nobody called to cancel. On my way to the hair salon, I got excited. Maybe this perm would happen after all. As I entered the salon, Diana came running to me saying: "Dr. Gilbert, your husband was here! As of 2 hours ago, I have no electricity in the salon! There is electricity everywhere else in the building and even in the bathroom but not in the salon! But you know what, this won't stop us, my boyfriend just brought me a generator. It won't be enough power to give us light but at least we'll have hot water which we need for a perm. We are going to do this today, Dr. Gilbert. We are!" I burst out laughing! I asked her for a few minutes of privacy. I went outside to talk to Steve and reassure him. I told him not to worry. It was going to be OK. In the past, I would always manage to convince him to do something I would really want, as long as it wasn't harmful or destructive. I would seduce him and promise him lots of good sex (I would always keep my promises) and he would always end up saying yes to whatever I wanted. He would never ever regret saying yes. This time, I tried doing the same thing. Only one problem, I couldn't promise him good sex anymore but I told him again how much I loved him. I came back in the salon and with the noisy generator at the background, Diana started rolling my hair. She managed to finish putting my hair in curlers and applied the perm stuff on it. I couldn't believe it! The perm was really going to happen today! Wahoo! What an accomplishment!

One hour later, I had a beautiful perm. I was time for a cut. Unfortunately, it was getting dark outside and the generator was not giving enough power for lights. We just had a few minutes left of daylight. We had to go outside on the balcony to catch those last few minutes. She only had time for a little trim, not a real haircut. That was OK. Steve would be happy because I still had long hair and I was happy because I had a beautiful perm. It was a good compromise. I went back home smiling and full of love for Steve, feeling his soul all around me.

I mentioned that I went to France to spend 2 and a half weeks with my mother who was 87 years old at the time and in great shape. I purposely went there because it was Steve's birthday and our anniversary. I didn't want to spend those days by myself. During that trip, I had a few signs from Steve. Here is what happened: The week of our anniversary, Mom and I flew to the South of France and rented a car to go and visit some older cousins. When we flew, we did it from airport gate # 13. The district of France we visited where the older cousins lived happened to be district # 13. We stayed in a hotel and I happened to have room # 113. Mom and I had lunches out all the time but only one dinner out. For that dinner, we had table # 13. I was wondering why we had that many 13. Was it a sign from Steve? What did that mean? Suddenly it struck me! It was our 13th year anniversary! I was stunned! Tears rolled down my cheeks.

One day in France, I specifically called Steve to help me. I was driving from Aix-en-Provence to Roquebrune Cap-Martin. After a few hours of driving, I felt very tired. I needed a break from driving and it was time for lunch. I drove down to the little town of Villefranche-sur-mer near the ocean. I found a restaurant facing the little harbor. Now I only needed a place to park. I had forgotten how narrow French streets were. I got into a long very narrow street that ended up being a dead end. People were parked everywhere (like French people usually do) and there was no parking spot anywhere. There was barely a small space to turn around and even though there was only space for a one way traffic, it was a two way street. I had no idea how to get out of where I was, no idea how to find a parking spot around the restaurant, I was exhausted and hungry. Mom next to me was getting anxious and very hungry too. I was miserable. I called Steve: "Steve, help! Can you do something for me please?" I really wasn't expecting any response when suddenly, I heard a woman calling me. She was walking in the street towards me: "You look like you are in trouble! I am parked right here. It is a really good spot and very easy to get in and out. I have to leave and you can take my spot." I just couldn't believe it! Steve had found a way! I thanked him profusely!

After parking, Mom and I walked to the restaurant. It was completely packed with not one single table available. Waiters and waitresses were busy running around. Suddenly as I was looking more closely, I saw a little table set for 2 people on the terrace directly facing the harbor. That table looked like a little oasis in the middle of a busy restaurant. I asked if we could use it. The waiter said yes! It was available! I took it as a sign from Steve again! As Mom and I sat down at the table, a beautiful leaf, blown by the wind, went flying down from a nearby tree and landed right in front of me on my plate! I had tears in my eyes! I knew it was from Steve, my wonderful husband, the Love of my Life!

# Chapter 32
# My advice to all of you.

Today, I am very aware of my own mortality and I don't take anything for granted. I spend quality time with my wonderful mother, mother-in-law, Steve's brothers and sisters and their families. I spend quality time with my awesome nieces and nephews. I am in close contact with my very dear cousin Evelyn, my best friends Richard and Christine, my precious friends from all over the world and my very helpful neighbors. Although I miss Steve a lot, I am making the conscious effort to look at what I have in my life and not what I have lost. I fall asleep every night thanking God for all the joys I've had in the last 50 years of my life. I wake up every morning amazed that I am still alive, that I can see, hear, touch, taste, smell, use both my hands and feet and have no pain anywhere in my body. I am truly appreciating my journey on earth, enjoying the simple joys of the "here and now", aware of not knowing what is around the corner of the road I am on.

With this book, I am hoping to touch you, the reader. I want to show you how my life has shaped me to be the person I am now. I want to tell you my adventures and show you my mistakes. Hopefully this way, you will learn from them and will not make the same ones. I want to show you how I fell and how I got back on my feet stronger than ever before. I want to teach you never to take anything for granted. Yes, money is important but far more important than money are health and happiness. I'll have reached my goal of touching part of you if after reading this book, you start appreciating the real value of having a warm heated home and enough hot water to enjoy a hot bath. Appreciate the balanced and delicious food you eat, take the time to go for a walk everyday, stop to smell the flowers on your way, appreciate being able to sleep at night without pain, appreciate this beautiful and perfect body of yours with its stunning complexity! Don't take your good health for granted! One day, your body will fail you and that is when you will realize how much you had and how much you lost. Start appreciating your wonderful body now! Appreciate listening to your perfect breath, appreciate slowly moving your arms, legs, fingers and toes without pain. Appreciate the fact that your eyes can see the beautiful scenery around you. Blind people will tell you how lucky you are. Appreciate the fact that your ears can listen to music and hear sounds around you. When you'll be older, you might not hear as well any more.

It you have medical problems, don't hesitate to get a second, third and maybe 4th medical opinion like I did for my family. Remember that every physician might have a different solution for you. Remember that there are a lot of medical mistakes being made. Double check everything. Don't trust anybody. Always ask for your own personal copy of your blood result, X-Ray or CT scan. Keep a copy of your file at home. Yes, it is perplexing that I, a physician, am telling you not to trust any physician. I am only trying to protect you. Most physicians are overworked and stressed out. Even though most are excellent, they can always overlook something and even the best ones can make medical mistakes. The advantage of getting several opinions on your problem is that you'll most likely avoid medical mistakes and you'll get a choice of solutions. This way, you can choose the one that seems the most appropriate for you.

Find your calling in life like I did. Life is too short to live it without passion. Find what you are passionate about and spend time exploring it. Living your passion will bring you strength and health. Try to find a job that includes it. If this isn't possible, keep it as a hobby but always be open to the possibility of finding another job that includes your passion.

As far as relationships go, don't hesitate to get out of unhealthy relationships. They are destructive. They will weaken you and your health will start failing you. Your perfect mate exists somewhere on this earth. You just need to know yourself well enough to decide who you need as a mate. Then, you need to make the effort to find him or her. In my life, I have worked hard to get every single thing I wanted. I have put a lot of effort into finding my wonderful husband. You might need to do the same thing. Remember, love is not as simple as it seems. You need to be compatible emotionally, physically, sexually, financially, religiously, spiritually and intellectually. You need to agree on how many children to have and how to raise them. You need to agree on how to take care of your parents. If you succeed in all this, it will be a great example for your children and your friends. It will show and teach everybody that true happiness is attainable. Everybody will want to imitate you and it will be truly wonderful. If you settle for less, it will teach your children that they can settle for less too. If you stay with an abusive mate, your children will accept an abusive mate too. They will not know that they deserve better. A healthy relationship will be so foreign to them that it will scare them away. They will be drawn to an abusive relationship which will feel familiar and safe and they will need counseling, and perhaps psychotherapy, for the rest of their life to change this.

Once you have found your mate, do everything you can to make him or her as happy as possible. I recommend the kind of relationship my husband Steve and I had. We admired and respected each other immensely. I listened to his problems and he listened to mine. We did our best to try to fix them. We talked about everything and made each other laugh from our jokes. I cooked and baked his favorite meals and desserts while he fixed up the house. We kissed and hugged several times a day. We cuddled every night before falling asleep, thanking each other for all the things the other one did and telling how much we loved each other. Our love making was always wonderful because we always tried to make the other one happy. We were always direct and honest with each other, never hiding any feeling. That's the kind of fulfilling relationship I recommend.

Know that whatever you do will influence the life of your children. Spend time with them, give them as much unconditional love as possible and teach them the difference between right and wrong. Remember that those first 18 years spent with them are crucial. You need to give and teach them everything without expecting anything back. The act of giving is the most rewarding. If you expect to receive anything back, you will be disappointed if it doesn't happen. If you don't expect anything back, everything you'll receive will be wonderful.

Give love to your parents like I gave love to mine and spend quality time with them. Remember that Moms need to be listened to and understood. Don't criticize them too much. If they haven't changed until now, they will probably not change any more. Accept your parents the way they are. Appreciate what they have given you and be thankful. Be as helpful as you can at the end of their life. They are getting older and are scared. They need you to listen to them, to reassure them and love them. With your help, they will leave our world peacefully and this peace will stay with you for the rest of your own life.

Follow in my footsteps: Give love to your friends and acquaintances. Always do the right thing. Respect others, whoever they are. There again, give without expecting anything back from anybody. Everybody deserves love and respect. It could be a person who has lost everything and lives in a refugee camp or an extremely rich successful person in a mansion. It could be somebody coming out of prison or a homeless person on a street. If somebody's answer is aggressive and negative, don't take it personally. It only means that he or she is having a bad day. Some people lived a very painful life. Their answer could sometimes be negative. It usually has nothing to do with you. Keep on doing the right thing and spread love. Give without expecting anything back.

Last but not least, remember that ultimately this is your very own precious life. Appreciate it!!! Life is short! Spend as little time as possible with negative thoughts, arguing with people or complaining about things. It is a waste of precious minutes. Focus on the positive aspects of things. Focus and be thankful for what you have even if you have very little.

Life needs to be appreciated now, this minute, this second. You are given the most priceless wonderful gift every day. You are given 1440 precious minutes per day. Make the best of those and teach others to do the same!!!

As for me, I am doing exactly what I am preaching. All I know is that I am appreciating every single minute of my life. I am full of Love for my family, my patients, nature, animals, for my body and for the human race.

I don't know what my future will be but whatever it is, I am welcoming it with open arms.

# *The End*